Georg Gresley Perry

The Christian Fathers

Georg Gresley Perry

The Christian Fathers

ISBN/EAN: 9783337022709

Printed in Europe, USA, Canada, Australia, Japan

Cover: Foto ©Lupo / pixelio.de

More available books at **www.hansebooks.com**

THE CHRISTIAN FATHERS.

BY

GEORGE G. PERRY, M.A.,

Prebendary of Lincoln, &c.

PUBLISHED UNDER THE DIRECTION OF THE
TRACT COMMITTEE.

LONDON:
SOCIETY FOR PROMOTING CHRISTIAN KNOWLEDGE.

SOLD AT THE DEPOSITORIES:
77, GREAT QUEEN STREET, LINCOLN'S INN FIELDS;
4, ROYAL EXCHANGE; 48, PICCADILLY;
AND BY ALL BOOKSELLERS.

LIVES
OF THE
EARLY FATHERS.

ST. IGNATIUS.

WHEN the rulers of the world were heathen, and haters of the pure religion of Christ, the way in which Christian constancy and devotion had to be shown was the way of martyrdom. From the time of St. Stephen, who was the first to seal his testimony with his blood, down to the age of Constantine, a period of nearly 300 years, persecutions of the Christians prevailed more or less throughout the great Roman empire. We have records of the sufferings and triumphant death of many of these martyrs, but thousands perished of whom we do not even know the names, but who are not forgotten by Him whom they loved even to the death. Among the more distinguished Christian martyrs, the accounts of whom have happily been preserved for us, one of the earliest and most illustrious was Ignatius, Bishop of Antioch. We have only to turn to the Acts of the Apostles to see how important a place in the early history of Christianity the great city of Antioch was. Large numbers of Christians were found there in the very first days of the Gospel.* It was here that the name of "Christians" † was first given to the disciples of Jesus, and the great Apostle Paul made this, the capital of Syria, his head-quarters for several years; while from thence he, with his fellow-labourers, spread the word of God through Asia Minor and Greece. The labours of St. Paul were specially addressed to the Gentiles at Antioch, but St. Peter, whose work lay principally among the Jews, also visited Antioch, and made a large number of converts there. Ignatius, of whom we come now to speak, was well known to both these Apostles. We are told by Chrysostom that he was "nursed up by the Apostles, and made partaker both of their familiar discourses and of their more secret

* Acts xi. 21. † Acts xi. 26.

and advanced teaching." We have also the best authority for saying that he was well known to St. John; so that it is impossible to conceive anyone having a more perfect Christian training than he had. So well did he profit by this divine instruction, and such devotion did he show to the cause of Christ, that he was selected, probably by St. Paul himself, to be the first bishop of the important Church of Antioch.

Antioch contained at this time more than 200,000 souls. There were many Christian converts, both Jews and Gentiles; as these did not agree together in every point, the Apostles thought it best that each section of the Church should have its bishop. Thus Euodius was appointed by St. Peter as bishop of the Jewish Christians, and Ignatius by St. Paul, bishop of the Gentile Christians. At the death, however, of Euodius, the Christians, both Jewish and Gentile, having now learned to be of one mind, Ignatius succeeded to the sole charge, and for the long period of forty years governed his important diocese with the greatest prudence and devotion. During that period persecution was frequently raging, but Ignatius was ever anxious to withdraw his flock from danger if possible, and not to encourage them in any way to court martyrdom —as some of the early Christians did. " He governed the Church with zeal," says a contemporary, who wrote an account of his martyrdom; " with difficulty leading them through those storms in old days which came upon them in the persecutions of Domitian; like a good pilot, using the rudder of prayer and fasting, and with continual teaching, and a spirit ever bold and constant, he opposed the storm, fearing lest perchance he should lose some of the more timid and simple. He rejoiced, therefore, when the Church was left in quiet, and there was a slight cessation from the persecution."* This passage gives us a general impression of the prudence as well as of the zeal of the good bishop, but unfortunately history has not preserved the record of any facts connected with the discharge of his high office. We can only gather, from what we are told of him afterwards, and from the tone of his letters written to other Churches, how intense must have been his devotion to his work. These letters were not, indeed, written until he was on his way to martyrdom, as we shall presently relate; but as they are most interesting in showing us the mind

* Martyr. S. Ignatii., Pat. Apost. vol. 2.

of this holy man, we will give a few extracts from them before we tell of his glorious death.

The Ephesian Church we find had sent to him Onesimus,* their bishop, to comfort him in his troubles, and he returned them a letter full of gratitude and Christian love. "In every way," he writes, "ought we to glorify Jesus Christ who hath glorified us," and especially by humble subjection to our spiritual rulers. "And let us pray for all men without ceasing, for there is ever a hope of their obtaining repentance. Suffer them also to gain instruction from your works. Reply to their anger by meekness; to their great words by being of an humble spirit; answer their blasphemies by prayers; their errors by being firm in the faith; their fierceness by mildness; being not imitators of them, but imitators of the Lord." . . . "Be zealous to be more frequent in your public assemblies for giving thanks and glory to God, for by frequent meetings the power of Satan is destroyed, and his destructiveness is weakened by your being of one mind in the faith." . . . "It is better to keep silence and really to be, than to talk and not to be. Teaching is

---

* The same person mentioned by St. Paul in the Epistle to Philemon.

good, if he that teaches also acts." Writing to the Magnesian Church, he uses this striking simile: "There are two coins, one the coin of God, the other the coin of the world, and each of them has its own special impression upon it. The unbelievers use the coin of this world, but those whose faith worketh by love, use the coin which has the impression upon it of God the Father through Jesus Christ."

To the Church of the Trallians he writes: "I have many high thoughts in God, but I measure myself, lest I should be destroyed by boasting; for now ought I the more to fear, and not to give heed to those who would puff me up, for they who thus speak to me do but inflict stripes upon me. For I indeed welcome suffering, but I know not whether I am worthy. The envy of the enemy of souls is not seen by many, but his attacks are felt by me. I long, therefore, for meekness, by which the power of the ruler of this world is broken."

The deep humility which is apparent in these words is further shown in a passage in his letter to the Roman Church: "Remember in your prayers that Church in Syria, which now, as I am removed, has God alone for its pastor; Jesus

Christ will watch over it as bishop, and your love will help it. I indeed am ashamed to have the name of their bishop, being not worthy, but the very least of them all, and an offscouring; but I have obtained mercy to be somewhat if I may but win God." The views of Ignatius on the duties of a bishop may be seen in the letter which he wrote to Polycarp, his beloved friend, the bishop of Smyrna. "I exhort you in all love," he writes, "with which you yourself are furnished, to apply earnestly to your work, and to exhort all that they may be saved. Justify your high post by the unceasing care which you take both for the temporal and spiritual welfare of your people. Be mindful of unity, than which nothing is more precious. Support all, as the Lord supports you. Bear with all in love, as also you do, pray for greater wisdom than you possess. Be vigilant, keeping a spirit which slumbereth not. Converse with each separately, so as to bring them help from God. Support the diseases of all as a perfect champion of the faith, knowing that where the toil is greater, here is great reward."

These extracts will give an idea of the spirit in which Ignatius executed his office as bishop of Antioch. But we are not left to judge of his character by his words alone. He who wrote these things to others, could also show in his own life, and by the most searching of tests, that these high and exalted sentiments were the cherished feelings of his own heart. It was about the year 107 A.D., when Trajan, the Emperor, elated with his victory over the Scythians and the Daci, came to Antioch to make preparations for his war against the Parthians. "He held," says the ancient Christian writer, "that his triumph was as yet but defective, so long as the God-fearing band of Christians was unsubdued and refused to join with the rest of his people in the worship of the false gods, and he threatened them with a terrible persecution which should compel them either to purchase their lives by sacrificing to the false gods, or should doom them to death." When the powerful Emperor had established himself in Antioch, with a determination to carry out this terrible purpose, we can imagine how deeply the soul of the holy Ignatius must have been grieved thereby. He thought of his beloved flock threatened with torture and death; and for some of them, too, he doubtless feared lest their faith should not prove strong enough to resist the terrors of persecution, and lest they should turn their backs upon their Lord and do sacrifice to the heathen gods. Moved by these anxious feelings and fears, he judged it to be the best and wisest part for him, who was the chief pastor of the threatened Church, of his own accord to put himself forward, and by this voluntary offering perhaps to appease the fury of the Emperor, and to save his people from the trials which threatened them. In this spirit of devoted Christian love, and not in the proud spirit of one who coveted martyrdom for his own glory, the venerable bishop sought the presence of the heathen Emperor. On his appearing before him, he was assailed with bitter words:—" Who art thou, possessed by an evil spirit, who art so eager to transgress our ordinances, and persuadest others also to their destruction?" Ignatius replied, "None can call him who bears the Lord * possessed by evil spirits, for the devils fly from the servants of the Lord. Having Christ for my heavenly King, I destroy the wiles of the evil spirits."

"*Trajan.* Who is this 'bearer of the Lord?'

* Ignatius was known among the Christians by the name Theophorus, the " bearer of the Lord."

"*Ignatius.* He that hath Christ in his breast.

"*Trajan.* Do you not think then that we have gods within us, we who have their help against our enemies?

"*Ignatius.* You are in error in calling the evil deities of the heathen gods; for there is one God, who made heaven and earth and the sea and all that in them is, and one Christ Jesus, the only begotten Son of God, in whose kingdom may I have a place.

"*Trajan.* Meanest thou Him who was crucified under Pontius Pilate?

"*Ignatius.* I mean Him that nailed to the cross my sin with the author of it, and who has thrown down under the feet of them that bear Him in their hearts all the error and wickedness of devils.

"*Trajan.* Dost thou then carry in thyself the Crucified One?

"*Ignatius.* I do, for it is written 'I will dwell in them and walk in them.' *

"*Trajan.* We give sentence that Ignatius, who says that he bears in himself the Crucified One, shall be put in chains by soldiers and taken

* 2 Cor. vi. 16.

to great Rome to be made the food of wild beasts for the gratification of the people.

"*Ignatius.* I give thanks to thee, O Lord and Master, because thou hast deigned to honour me with perfect love in allowing me to be bound, as Thy apostle Paul was, in iron chains."

Thus saying, he cheerfully embraced his chains, and having prayed for his Church, and commended it with tears to the care of the Most High, like some noble victim, the leader of a gallant flock, he was hurried away on his journey to Rome to be thrown to the savage beasts. Being consigned to a guard of ten soldiers, he took leave of his beloved Antioch (and a sad parting, no doubt, there was between him and his people, who were to see his face no more), and was conducted on foot to Seleucia, a port of Syria about sixteen miles distant from Antioch, the very place where Paul and Barnabas set sail for Cyprus.* Here going on board ship, after a tedious and difficult voyage, they arrived at Smyrna, a famous city of Ionia, where Ignatius was permitted to see Polycarp, bishop of that place, his old fellow-pupil under St. John the Apostle. Joyful was the meeting of these two holy men; Polycarp

* Acts xiii. 4.

even rejoicing in the condemnation of Ignatius as a glorious witness for Christ, and exhorting him to constancy unto the end. From all the province of Asia, which, even at that early period, was full of Christians, there came bishops, priests, and deacons to see the venerable bishop who was about to seal his testimony with his blood. To them and to their Churches the holy Ignatius wrote those letters of his which have been preserved in an imperfect form, and from which we have already made some extracts. He also wrote a letter at this time to the Christians at Rome, to acquaint them with his state, and his longing desire for martyrdom, and to entreat them not to pray that he might be spared the trial, but rather that he might be able to bear a good witness for Christ therein.

"I am afraid," he says, "of your love, lest it should do me a wrong, for to you it is easy to do what ye will; but to me it is hard to win God, if ye will seek to deliver me. If ye will keep silence in my case, then shall I be accepted of God; but if, out of love to my person, ye pray for my safety, then shall I have to run again. I write to all the Churches, and tell them that I am willing to die for God, if ye will not hinder me. I beseech you be not towards me full of misplaced kindness. Suffer me to be the food of the wild beasts, through which I may win God. I am God's corn, and I would be ground by the teeth of the wild beasts, that I may be found the pure bread of Christ." Such eagerness for martyrdom, even in its most terrible form, shows us how entirely the religious spirit had swallowed up and moulded into itself all the other faculties and powers of nature. Here indeed was a mighty example of the strength of the grace of Christ.

After a stay of some time at Smyrna, Ignatius and his guards set sail for Troas, another city where the saint would be on the track of that beloved Apostle Paul who had appointed him to his work at Antioch. And in this track they continued to follow, crossing the sea from Troas to Neapolis, and going from thence to Philippi, as St. Paul had done. At Philippi, as we learn from a letter of St. Polycarp, Ignatius was treated with the greatest kindness and courtesy, and was conducted on his journey on foot through Macedonia and Epirus to Epidamnus, a city of Dalmatia. Here again they took ship and sailed down the Adriatic to Rhegium, on the very extreme point of Italy, and thence northwards along the Italian coast to Puteoli. Ignatius would fain have landed here, as St. Paul had done, and have entered Rome by land; but a strong favourable wind blowing, the ship went on her course, and quickly arrived at the mouth of the Tiber, from whence was only a journey of sixteen miles to Rome.

The Christians hearing of the coming of Ignatius, crowded out to meet him, and to receive him with every demonstration of respect and sympathy. Terrible as was the danger for all who were known to be Christians, yet these brave men were ready to incur it, rather than suffer one who had witnessed so good a confession, and was of such high character among Christians, to enter the great city without a due tribute of their admiration and love. Ignatius received their greetings with affectionate gratitude, but he still continued to press upon them that which he had insisted on in his letter, that they should not "grudge him to God," nor strive to avert his fate by their prayers, but only pray for his perfect consummation. The holy man was at once conducted to the prefect of the city, and, the Emperor's letters having been read, he was adjudged to die at one of the solemn festivals of the people which was near at hand. At these festivals the amusements provided by the Em-

ST. IGNATIUS' MARTYRDOM.—*Page* 19.

perors for the people consisted in the bloody and desperate conflicts of gladiators who were criminals or prisoners of war, condemned to fight with one another until one should be slain, and in the savage fury of wild beasts let loose upon wretched men and women sentenced to death.

It is difficult to conceive how such sights could have been witnessed by vast crowds without shrinking, and even with pleasure and amusement; and the fact that they were thus witnessed is a strong proof of the *unnatural* state into which a false religion and a life of unchecked licentiousness bring the human heart. The valiant martyr, Ignatius, shrank not for a moment from the dreadful death which was prepared for him. He repeated the words already quoted, that he was "God's own corn, now to be ground, that he might become the pure bread of Christ," and the hungry lions, rushing upon him, quickly carried out that which was his most ardent desire and prayer. The bones which remained after the beasts had satisfied their hunger upon the holy martyr were collected by the faithful deacons who had followed his footsteps all the way, who witnessed his sufferings and afterwards compiled a plain and truthful account of his martyrdom, and were conveyed by them back to Antioch, where they were honourably buried.

Almost immediately after the death of Ignatius, the Emperor Trajan stopped the persecution against the Christians which he had begun. There are some who assert that having heard a full account of the sufferings of this holy man, and how undauntedly he had undergone that bitter death, Trajan repented of what he had done. If this were so, Ignatius, as an ancient writer observes, was not only in his life a great benefactor of the Christian name, but in his death also was the procurer of much good for the religion of Christ.

ST. POLYCARP.

Polycarp was born towards the latter part of the reign of Nero, the Roman emperor, and probably at Smyrna, a city of Ionia in Asia Minor, which boasted to be the chief and most splendid city of the Roman province of Asia, both for beauty and size. In his early youth he is said to have been educated and supported by a pious woman named Callisto, and we have very good authority for saying that he was taught by the holy Apostle St. John, and that he had the privilege of conversing with many who had seen our Lord in the flesh.

The name of the Bishop of Smyrna, when Polycarp grew up, was Bucolus. By him Polycarp was admitted into holy orders, being ordained deacon and catechist or teacher of the Church. Bucolus, we read, had always predicted that Polycarp would succeed him in his office, and so it turned out, for at his death Polycarp was appointed by St. John to be the bishop to succeed him—a great and notable trust, and one certain to be attended with danger, if not death, in those days of bitter persecution of the faith of Christ.

We have seen, in the life of St. Ignatius, that Polycarp was in office as bishop when that holy martyr was conducted to Smyrna on his way to Rome; and the beautiful and affectionate letter written soon after his leaving Smyrna to Polycarp, by Ignatius, shows how greatly he was prized by the martyr. He recommended to Polycarp the care of his Church at Antioch, from which he was being torn away, knowing him (as Eusebius, the historian of the early Church, tells us) to be truly an apostolical man, and being assured that he would use his utmost care and fidelity in the matter.

But we have a still more certain testimony of the estimation due to the character of Polycarp. We can turn to the Scripture itself and see how the Apostle St. John is commissioned to write of this bishop. It is supposed, with much probability, that the "Angel of the Church in Smyrna," of whom the Apostle speaks in the second chapter of the Book of Revelation, could have been none other than St. Polycarp. How, then, does the inspired writer set forth the message from his Lord to him: "Unto the Angel of the Church in Smyrna write: These things saith the first and the last, which was dead, and is alive. I know thy works, and tribulation and poverty (but thou art rich), and I know the blasphemy of them which say they are Jews, and are not, but are the synagogue of Satan. Fear none of those things which thou shalt suffer: behold the devil shall cast some of you into prison that ye may be tried; and ye shall have tribulation ten days: be thou faithful unto death and I will give thee a crown of life."*

These divine words describe the Bishop of Smyrna as rich in faith and Christian grace, as unmoved in the midst of tribulation and poverty, and as going onwards towards a glorious consummation of his course, being faithful unto death, and thus winning a crown of life. There cannot be any one among the early fathers of the Church more worthy of our interest than he who is thus divinely commended. How much, therefore, is it to be lamented that we have not fuller records of the life of Polycarp at Smyrna, and that in his case, as in that of Ignatius, it is only in the triumphant close of

* Rev. ii. 9, 10.

his life that we have him clearly brought before us. That his administration of his diocese was perplexed by the false opinions of heretics we gather from St. John's words. There were among his people Judaizing Christians, who had not the true spirit of the Jew as described by St. Paul in his Epistle to the Romans.* We also know from the letter of Ignatius that a sect called the Docetæ were very troublesome at Smyrna. These men taught that our Lord Jesus Christ only suffered on the cross and rose again in *appearance*, not in reality; that His human body was a phantom which deceived the eyes of His enemies.

Against such destructive notions Ignatius warns the Smyrneans with all earnestness, and we may imagine how the prevalence of such opinions must have pained Polycarp, who is exhorted by Ignatius specially to labour for unity, and not to be afraid of those who seem to be of importance but who do not teach the truth, but to stand firm against them like an anvil which yields not to the blows of the hammer. These heretics were far more dreaded by the early fathers than the heathen persecutors. They regarded the latter as those who had only the power to kill

* Rom. ii. 28, 29.

the body, but the others as those who endangered the soul. Being very zealous to keep the faith intact as it had been handed to them by the Apostles, they were careful about matters even apparently of smaller importance than those which touched the reality of the Saviour's work. A dispute arose very early in the history of the Church whether the great festival of Easter should be kept always on the Lord's day, and thus on varying days of the month, or whether it should follow the computation of the Jewish feast of the Passover, and thus fall always on the fourteenth day of the month, but not always on the same day of the week. There was much to be urged by way of reasons on both sides of the question, and the partisans of both arrangements declared that they had apostolic authority. The Eastern Christians generally followed the calculation which made the day of the month the important part, and thus were called Quartodecimans, or the "favourers of the fourteenth;" while the Westerns preferred to make the day of the week the determining point, thinking it unfitting that this great festival, which in fact fixed the first day of the week as the Christian holy day, should be celebrated on any other day than the first. We may easily see that the matter was by no means a trifling one, as some writers would have us to suppose. If it was important that the Christians should be at unity among themselves, and that they should show to the heathen the same firm and united appearance on all sides, then was it important that they should not be seen engaged in celebrating their highest festival at different times, as though they were practically disunited. It was the sense of the great importance of the matter which led Polycarp to leave his beloved flock at Smyrna and to undertake a long journey to Rome to confer with the bishop there about this subject. Polycarp favoured the day of the month calculation, which he said he had learned from St. John, while the Roman Church, which was now beginning to be an important part of the Christian world, favoured the arrangement for the first day of the week. The account of Polycarp's visit to Rome, which has been left us by Irenæus, gives us a most pleasing glance at the internal state of the Christian Church in those early days. Anicetus was Bishop of Rome at that time. He received Polycarp affectionately, and they had many conferences about the disputed point. Neither would yield their opinion, but they both agreed that the essence of Christianity did not consist in these things, but in the devotion of the heart to their common Lord and in true love of the brethren. In token of this they joined together in the Holy Eucharist, and Anicetus, to do honour to Polycarp, and to show his complete union with him, insisted on Polycarp consecrating the elements in his church.

These good men had no difficulty in joining together in Christian worship, although each continued to maintain his own opinions as to the points disputed between them. The history of the Church is far too full of records of quite a different temper in those who held opposing views on religious matters. Polycarp, during his stay in Rome, set himself to convince gainsayers, testifying the truth of those doctrines which he had received from the Apostles. By these means he wrought upon many and reclaimed them to the Church, for the evil heresies of self-willed teachers had already produced much evil, and many had separated themselves from the faith once delivered to the saints.

Among the most dangerous and mischievous of

these false teachers was Marcion, who had propounded doctrines utterly subversive of Christian truth. This man one day meeting Polycarp in the street, and not receiving from him the greeting which he had expected, called out "Polycarp, own us!" Upon which Polycarp immediately answered, "I own thee indeed as the first-born of Satan."

This is recorded by Irenæus, who knew Polycarp in his latter days, and speaks with the greatest admiration of his fervent zeal for the truth.* He also tells us of an anecdote which Polycarp was wont to relate of the Apostle St. John. St. John had one day gone to a bath in Ephesus, but when he entered he saw in the bath Cerinthus, another of the chief leaders of the Gnostic heresy. Upon seeing him he immediately hastened out of the bath, exclaiming, "Let us fly, lest the bath should fall on us." For what guilt could be greater than that of those who poisoned, by their admixture of "knowledge falsely so-called," the holy truth which our Lord and His Apostles had preached to the world. In the epistle which Polycarp himself addressed to the Philippian Church, we have this strongly in-

* Eusebius, iv. 14.

sisted on. "Every one who doth not acknowledge that Jesus Christ is come in the flesh is Antichrist;* and he who will not acknowledge the witness of the cross is of the devil; and he who perverts the oracles of the Lord to his own lusts, and says that there is neither resurrection † nor judgment, this man is the first-born of Satan. Wherefore, leaving the folly of the many, and their false teachings, let us turn to the Word which was delivered to us at the beginning, giving ourselves to fasting and prayers continually, supplicating the all-seeing God not to lead us into temptation, according as the Lord spake, 'The spirit indeed is willing, but the flesh is weak.' ‡ Let us continue without ceasing in our hope, and in the earnest of our justification, which is Jesus Christ, 'Who His own self bare our sins in His own body on the tree;' § ' Who did no sin, neither was guile found in His mouth,' ‖ but bare all things for us that we might live by Him. Let us imitate His patience; and if we suffer for His name, let us glorify Him, for this is the example which He hath given us in Himself, and this we have accepted by faith."

* 1 John iv. 3. † See 1 Cor. xv. 12.
‡ Matt. xxvi. 41. § 1 Pet. ii. 24. ‖ 1 Pet. ii. 22.

An intensely scriptural tone breathes through this epistle to the Philippians. He seems to condemn heresies in the very language of St. Paul, St. Peter, and St. John; and the earnest way in which he exhorted the Philippians to meditate upon and cherish the epistle which St. Paul had written to them, shows how he loved the inspired teaching of the Apostles. "I remember," says Irenæus, "the very place in which he was wont to discourse, his going out and coming in, and all the character of his life. I can recall his personal appearance and the discourses he was wont to make to the people; and how he told us of his familiar intercourse with St. John and the others who had seen the Lord; and how he recounted their words and what he had heard from them concerning the Lord, His miracles and His teaching. These things, as one who had received them from those who were eye-witnesses of the Word of Life, Polycarp related exactly in accordance with the Scriptures. These things, through the mercy of God, I listened to with all zeal, making notes of them, not on paper, but in my heart, and still, through the grace of God, do I retain them exactly in my memory. I am able to bear witness before God that if he, the blessed and apostolical presbyter, heard any heretical doctrine, he would cry out and stop his ears and say, as was his wont, 'O glorious God, into what times hast Thou preserved me, that I should have to endure these things!' and he would fly away from the spot in which he had been sitting or standing when he heard these words. The same also is clear from the epistles which he sent to neighbouring Churches to encourage them, and those which he sent to some of the brethren to admonish and convert them."[*] We can easily understand the high value to the Church of this extreme love of the truth and hatred of error in those who formed, as it were, the connecting link between the Apostles and the ordinary pastors of the Church. Watching with jealous eye the importation of new doctrine, and pointing in all their writings to the Scriptures and the example of the Apostles as the sole source of truth, they laid up, by God's good providence, a great treasury of weapons fitted to use against error in every age.

But it was now the will of Him whom Polycarp served with his whole heart, that the Bishop of Smyrna, who had so long guided his flock by warn-

[*] Eusebius, v. 20.

ing and oral teaching, should give, by example, a still more glorious witness to the truth. His "faithfulness unto death" was now to be proved, and the "crown of life" which the Apostle had promised him in the name of his Saviour was now to reward him.

Happily we possess a detailed, and in every way credible, account of the martyrdom of this holy man, which we shall now give, observing only by the way that the words relating to the Church of Smyrna in the Apocalypse are exactly borne out by it. "A piece it is," says Dr. Cave, "that challenges a singular esteem and reverence, both for the subject matter and the antiquity of it, with which Scaliger thinks every serious and devout mind must needs be so affected as never to think it has enough of it; professing for his own part that he never met with anything in all the history of the Church with the reading whereof he was more transported, so that he seemed no longer to be himself." *

In the reign of M. Antoninus and L. Verus, Emperors of Rome, a severe persecution against the Christians began, and informers were encouraged by large bribes to denounce them, that they

* Cave's Lives of the Fathers, i. 118.

might be seized upon. This persecution increased still more when Antoninus, intending to make an expedition against a warlike people, called together the heathen priests at Rome to celebrate solemn sacrifices to their gods to procure success for his expedition. The priests took occasion to assure the Emperor that the most acceptable offering he could make to the gods would be the complete destruction of the Christians, who everywhere despised their worship. The Emperor gave orders that it should be as they desired, and throughout his vast dominions the Christians were seized and brought to execution. At Smyrna, according as St. John had predicted, the persecution was severely felt. "Blessed and noble," says the Epistle of the Church of Smyrna, "were all those martyrdoms which took place according to the will of God—for we ought to be ever more and more cautious to ascribe to God the power over all things—for their noble spirit, and patience, and love of their Lord, who could fail to admire, who being torn with scourges, so that their flesh was laid bare down to the inmost veins and arteries, still endured, so that those who stood around were filled with pity and lamentation; but they were of so high a courage that none of them cried or groaned, showing to all of us that in the hour of their trial the martyrs of Christ are absent from the body, or rather that Christ stands by them and is present with them. Being occupied with the grace of Christ, they despised the trials of this world, purchasing for themselves in one short hour the freedom from eternal punishment; and thus the fire of their cruel tormentors was to them cool and refreshing. The most noble Germanicus strengthened the courage of others by his endurance, and gloriously contended with the beasts; for when the Governor would persuade him, and told him to have compassion upon his youth, he drew by force the beast towards him, desiring the more quickly to quit this life, in which injustice and wickedness so much prevailed. Whereupon all the multitude, wondering at the noble courage of the God-fearing race of the Christians, shouted out, "Away with the Atheists! Let Polycarp be sought for!"*

Polycarp had at first resolved to remain quietly at his post in expectation of martyrdom, but many of his flock urging him for their sakes to conceal himself, and reminding him of our

* Epistle of the Church of Smyrna, Pat. Apost. v. 2.

Lord's words, that when His followers were persecuted in one city they should flee into another,* he was prevailed upon to withdraw himself. Retiring to a neighbouring village with a few companions, he continued day and night in prayer for the Church and for those who were called upon to suffer. In the meantime, he was carefully sought for everywhere, and his friends persuaded him to retire to another village. Some suspicions as to the place of his concealment having reached the soldiers, they seized upon two youths, and having by stripes forced them to confess that they knew where he was, they compelled them to guide them to his place of concealment.

They came to the house when he was in bed at night, and he made no attempt to escape, saying, " The will of the Lord be done." When he heard that his persecutors were in the house, he came down to them with a cheerful countenance, and they were struck by the sight of this venerable man of so great age readily and even with smiles giving himself into their hands. By his orders, a feast was made for the soldiers in the house, and all that he asked of them was that he might have

---

* Matt. x. 23.

one hour for prayer. This was allowed him, and the holy man, betaking himself to his devotions, for two hours together poured forth such ardent prayers, that he seemed to all that heard him like one inspired. He was then set upon an ass and conducted into the city. Upon his way, he was met by one of the chief magistrates of the country, who making him come up into his chariot with him, did all he could, by crafty and smooth speeches, to make Polycarp consent to use a heathen prayer, and so to escape the danger which threatened him. But as Polycarp stedfastly refused to do this, the pretended kindness of the magistrate gave place to violence, and the aged Polycarp was rudely thrust out of the chariot so as to injure his thigh by the fall. Undisturbed by this, he hastened on as well as he was able to the place of execution, and appeared before the public tribunal, a great shout being raised by the mob in triumph that the head of the Christians was at length apprehended. In the midst of the tumult, it is said that a voice reached the ears of Polycarp, saying the words, "Be of good courage and play the man, Polycarp." The Proconsul or Governor seeing the aged man brought before him, asked if he were Polycarp. This being at once acknowledged, he then said: "Have some respect for your great age; swear by the genius of the Emperor. Repent, say 'Away with the impious.'"

Upon this Polycarp, looking round him with a severe countenance, and remembering the savage shouts with which these people had applauded the shedding of Christian blood, called out in a loud voice these words, but in a different sense, "Away with the impious." Then the Proconsul again bade him to swear by the heathen gods and to blaspheme Christ. The Saint replied: "Fourscore and six years have I served Him, and never did He any harm to me; how, then, shall I now blaspheme my King and Saviour?" "Swear," cried the Proconsul, "by the genius of the Emperor." Polycarp answered: "Since you are so vainly anxious that I should swear by the Emperor's genius, as you call it, as if you knew not who I am, hear my free confession. I am a Christian. If you would learn the Christian faith, appoint me a time and I will instruct you in it." The Proconsul advised him to try to persuade the people. He answered: "To you I rather choose to address my words, for we are commanded by the laws of our religion to give to princes and powers ordained of God all honour and reverence that is not against religion. For the people, I think them not fit judges to whom I should give an account of my faith."

The Proconsul now tried what threats would do. "I have wild beasts at hand," said he, "to whom I will cast thee unless thou repentest." "Call them," exclaimed the martyr, "for to us repentance from better to worse is impossible. It is good only to change from the bad to the good."

The Proconsul: "I will cause thee to be consumed by fire, if you despise the beasts, unless thou repentest."

Polycarp: "Thou threatenest a fire which can burn but for a season, and after a little time is quenched, for thou knowest nothing of the fire of the judgment to come and of eternal punishment, which is reserved for the impious. But why tarriest thou? Bring what thou wilt."

The boldness and eagerness of the martyr struck the Governor with amazement. He sent a herald into the midst of the throng to proclaim "Polycarp hath confessed himself to be a Christian," upon which the mob, composed of heathens and Jews, shouted aloud, "This is he that is the teacher of impiety; this is the father of the Christians; this is the destroyer of our gods; this is he who teaches many not to sacrifice nor to worship the gods." Then they clamorously demanded that Polycarp should be given to the lion. But the Governor refused, saying that the wild beast sports were over. Then they shouted that he should be burned. The Governor not opposing this, the savage mob quickly brought together faggots from the workshops and baths near at hand, the Jews being most conspicuous for their activity. A pile was soon raised, and the venerable bishop, casting aside his garments with all eagerness, mounted upon it. The officers were preparing to nail him to the stake, but he begged them to leave him free, assuring them that the Lord who supported him would give him strength to remain without flinching in the midst of the flames. Then, instead of nailing him, they only bound his hands. Upon this the martyr, ready now to be offered up as a sacrifice for the truth, poured forth, with eyes fixed upon heaven, the following prayer: "O Lord God Almighty, the Father of Thy well-beloved and ever blessed Son Jesus Christ, by whom we have received the knowledge of Thee; the God of angels, powers, and of every creature, and of the whole race of the righteous who live before Thee; I bless Thee that Thou hast condescended to bring me to this day and hour that I may receive a portion in the number of Thy holy martyrs, and drink of Christ's cup, for the resurrection to eternal life both of soul and body in the incorruptibleness of the holy Spirit. Into which number grant that I may be received this day, being found in Thy sight as a fair and acceptable sacrifice, such an one as Thou Thyself hast prepared, that so Thou mayest accomplish what Thou, O true and faithful God, hast foreshown. Wherefore I praise Thee for all Thy mercies, I bless Thee, I glorify Thee, through the eternal High-Priest Thy beloved Son Jesus Christ, with whom to Thyself and the Holy Ghost, be glory both now and for ever. Amen."

While the martyr thus prayed, the fire spread around him, but, to the astonishment of the beholders, it seemed not to touch his body but to envelop him like a sail inflated by the wind, while, to the brethren, who with excited devotion mingled among the crowd, there seemed to come a sweet perfume from his body. He was then, by command of the Governor, pierced with a sword, and again to the Christian eye-witnesses there

ST. POLYCARP'S MARTYRDOM.—*Page* 40

seemed to come forth such a vast amount of blood from his body as to quench the flames, while some thought that they saw a dove fly forth and wing its way to heaven, which they held to be the soul of the martyr. The Jews eagerly pressed upon the Governor to cause the body to be burned to ashes, and not to allow the Christians to have it for burial, lest, as they said, they should leave Christ and worship Polycarp, "Little considering," writes the author of the account of the martyrdom, " how impossible it is that either we should forsake Christ who died for the salvation of the whole world, or that we should worship any other. Him we adore as the Son of God; but martyrs, as the disciples and followers of our Lord, we deservedly love on account of their affection, which cannot be surpassed, towards their King and Master, with whom may it be our lot to become partakers and fellow-disciples." * At the same time that this holy man suffered death, others also suffered with him for the same holy cause, but no special account of them has been preserved. Polycarp is supposed to have reached the great age of one hundred years when he suffered, and

* Letter of the Church of Smyrna on St. Polycarp's martyrdom, Pat. Apost. ii. 563-611.

his martyrdom is held to have taken place in the year 167 A.D. The city where Polycarp bore such noble witness for the truth has long been under the sway of the unbeliever, and Christianity is still reviled and persecuted there, but the memory of the saint survives. The place where his ashes were buried is still known and reverenced by the Christians who live scattered among the Mahometans in Asia Minor, and traces of the Roman amphitheatre where he was executed are yet visible. We may hope and pray that the land where such noble witness was borne to the truth may yet be wholly reclaimed to be a portion of the holy Church of Christ.

ST. JUSTIN THE MARTYR.

WE now come to recount the history of one who was not only a holy martyr for the truth, by enduring death for the sake of his Lord, but also was a famous and unanswerable defender of it against the Jews and the heathens by his excellent and powerful writings. The writings of Ignatius and Polycarp were short practical addresses to the Christians themselves, but St. Justin aimed at victoriously establishing the truth of the Gospel to both Jew and Gentile, and refuting the vile calumnies which were spread abroad concerning the Christian Church, by showing it to be pure and spotless in its practice as well as true in its teaching. His writings happily remain, to prove to us the power of the Gospel to influence learned philosophers as well as simple and untaught men, and the account which he has given us of his conversion, through the mere love and search for truth, is a noble witness to the constraining power of Christianity over an honest and humble mind. Justin was born at Flavia Neapolis, in Palestine, the ancient Sichem of Samaria, of a Greek family, which had probably been sent there when the Roman Emperor Vespasian founded the colony. He was educated in the old heathen religion, and was carefully instructed in the learning and philosophy of the Gentile world, as his writings abundantly prove. In his youth he was sent to travel by way of acquiring knowledge, and among other places he visited Egypt, where, at Alexandria, he made particular enquiries about the famous seventy translators of the Hebrew Scriptures into Greek, and has given us an interesting account of what he heard concerning them. Enquiring about the tenets of the different sects of the philosophers, Justin was at length attracted to the Platonists, and became a disciple of their school.

How he was at length brought to a higher wisdom and a more perfect faith, he himself has told us in a most interesting manner, and we shall relate nearly in his own words: "Thinking I had now suddenly become wise by having discovered the philosophy of Plato, and desiring to meditate on it in solitude, I went into a field near to the sea-shore. Perceiving, however, that

I was followed by an old man of comely and grave appearance, I stopped and looked sharply at him. 'Do you know me?' said he. I declared that I did not. 'Why, then, do you look at me in that manner?' 'I am astonished,' I said, 'at seeing you here, for I did not expect to see anyone at this spot.' 'I am looking,' said he, 'for some of my friends. But what brings you here?' 'I delight,' said I, 'in solitary walks, where I can commune with myself and argue points.' 'Is it not better,' said he, 'to be a doer than a mere talker and arguer?' 'Of all employments,' said I, 'philosophy is the highest; and all other things are to be regarded as vastly inferior to it.' 'Can philosophy give happiness?' said he. 'Assuredly.' 'What, then, is the happiness which it gives?' 'The knowledge of the truth.' 'Can philosophy teach us the knowledge of God?' 'The soul has the power of contemplating and apprehending God.' 'But can the soul tell anything about the nature of God or about its own nature, and are not the sayings of philosophers on these points full of contradictions and absurdities?' 'It may be so; but to whom else are we to go for truth?' 'There are men far older than the philosophers who have spoken of these things, under the influence of the Holy Spirit of God. The truth of the claims of these men to speak as from God has been proved by the miracles which they wrought, and by their predictions which have come true in Christ. Do thou pray that the gates of light may be opened to thee, for all cannot understand these things, but only those to whom God and His Christ shall give understanding.'" With these words the old man left Justin, and he, much impressed by what he had heard, set himself earnestly to study the prophets and the writings of "the friends of Christ." In this way, said he, "I became indeed a philosopher, and would that all like me would follow the teaching of the Saviour, for it has indeed a terrible majesty to terrify those who have turned out of the right way, but to those who carefully observe it, it is the most sweet refreshment."*

The effect of Justin's enquiries into the truth of Christianity was greatly increased by his observation of the innocency of the lives of the Christians and the constancy of their deaths as martyrs. Thus, he says in his Apology addressed to the Roman Emperor: "For my own part, being yet

* Justin, Dial. cum Tryphone, Works, vol. ii. (Ed. Otto.)

detained under the Platonic teaching, when I heard the Christians traduced and reproached and yet saw them rushing fearlessly upon death, and venturing upon all those things that are accounted most dreadful and amazing to human nature, I concluded with myself that it was impossible that these men should walk on in vice and be carried away with the love of lust and pleasure. For what man that is a slave to pleasure and intemperance can cheerfully bid death welcome which he knows must put a period to all his pleasures and delights; and would not rather by all means endeavour to prolong his life as much as possible and to delude his adversaries, and conceal himself from the notice of the magistrates rather than voluntarily betray and offer himself to a present execution?"*

By the joint influence of what he saw and heard, and what he read for himself, Justin now became a sincere Christian about the year 133 A.D. In order to explain the grounds of this change to the Greeks, whose faith he had quitted, and to exhort them to follow his example, he wrote a treatise called "An exhortation to the Greeks," in which he displays, with much ridicule,

* Justin, Second Apology, c. 12.

the absurd nature of the religious opinions which the heathen cherished, and calls upon them to come to him "and partake of a most incomparable wisdom, and be instructed in a divine religion, and acquaint themselves with an immortal King."

Justin, after his conversion to Christianity, continued to wear the dress of a Greek philosopher. This was reasonable in him, as he considered himself now to have indeed reached the true philosophy, and as he constantly reminded his former friends and associates that such was the case. He now went to reside at Rome, as being the place where his learning and powers of writing could be of the greatest use in defending the Christian faith. Here he wrote treatises against all the heresies which were then distracting the Church, and in particular against Marcion, who was mentioned in the life of Polycarp, and who taught the most blasphemous doctrines.

But a still greater service to the Christian cause was performed by Justin at this time. Antoninus was then Emperor of Rome, a prince of a mild and kind disposition, who had published no persecuting edicts against the Christians. Nevertheless the Christians were generally persecuted and punished by the governors and magistrates of the empire under the edicts and laws passed by former Emperors. Justin thought that if the Emperor were properly informed of the real character of the Christians and their worship, how innocent their lives were, and how ready they were to act as good citizens and to perform all their duties, he would interfere to prevent the cruelties which were practised against them. Accordingly he set himself to compose, for the information of the Emperor, his "Apology for the Christians." This is a treatise of considerable length and full of the deepest interest, as giving us the most complete account of the way of life and the habits of those primitive disciples of the faith, who in those days of persecution adorned by their devotion and constancy the holy religion which they professed. We will extract some passages specially relating to the religious services of the early Christians:—

"I will now relate to you the manner in which we dedicate ourselves to God when we are renewed by Christ, that I may not, by omitting this, appear to have any sinister ends in my explanation. Whoever are persuaded of the truth of what we say and are ready to promise that they will live according to this, are taught by us to seek of God, with fasting and prayer, the remission of their former sins—we also praying and fasting with them. Then we lead them where there is water, and they are born anew in the same manner that we ourselves are. For in the name of God the Father and Ruler of all things, and of our Saviour Jesus Christ, and of the Holy Spirit, they are then bathed in the water. For Christ has said, 'Except ye be born again ye cannot enter into the kingdom of heaven.'* But it is clear to all that it is impossible for those who are once born to enter a second time into their mother's womb. And this reason for baptism we have learnt from the Apostles. Since, at our first birth, we were of necessity begotten in the natural way, and brought up in bad habits and evil courses, that we might not remain the children of wrath and ignorance, but of election and knowledge, and obtain remission of sins we had committed in the water, over him who chooses to be regenerate and repents of his sins, the name of God the Father and Ruler of all is pronounced. And this washing is called illumination, seeing that those who have learned these things are illumin-

* John iii 3.

ated in their minds, and in the name of Jesus Christ who was crucified under Pontius Pilate, and in the name of the Holy Spirit who foretold by the prophets all things relating to Jesus, he that is illuminated is washed." "After baptism we bring the convert to those who are called brethren, where they are assembled to make common prayer both for themselves and for him who has been illuminated, and for all others everywhere, earnestly beseeching that we may be thought worthy to learn what is true, and to be found in our works good and honest and careful guardians of the things enjoined to us, that we may obtain everlasting salvation. At the conclusion of our prayers we salute one another with a kiss. Then there is brought to the president of the brethren bread and a cup of water and wine, and he taking it gives glory to the Father of All, through the name of the Son and the Holy Ghost, and makes great thanksgiving for our being thought worthy of these things by Him. And at the end of these prayers and thanksgivings, all the people present shout forth their agreement, saying Amen, which means May it be so; and afterwards, those who are called by us Deacons give to each one who is present a portion of the bread and wine and water that has been blessed, and carry it away to those who are absent, and this food is called by us the Eucharist, of which it is not lawful for anyone to partake, except whosoever believes the things that we teach, and has been washed in that bath provided for the remission of sins and the new birth, and lives according to the commandment of Christ. For we do not hold these to be common bread and wine, but in the same way that Jesus Christ our Saviour being made flesh by the word of God took flesh and blood for our salvation, so have we been taught that this food, by which our blood and flesh are nourished when it is changed and digested, is, after it has been blessed by the saying of His prayer, the flesh and the blood of Jesus who was made flesh. For the Apostles, in their writings which are called Gospels, have handed it down that Jesus thus commanded them; namely, that He took bread, and when He had given thanks, said, 'This do in remembrance of Me. This is My body.' And the same way, when He had taken the cup and given thanks, He said, 'This is My blood,' and that He gave it to them to partake of. Of these things we continually put one another in remembrance, and we that are able assist all that are in want, and we are always in unity, and we bless the Creator of all things through his Son Jesus Christ and the Holy Spirit, for all things that we are supplied with." "And on the day that is called Sunday, an assembly is made of all who dwell either in the city or the country, and the memorials of the Apostles and the writings of the prophets are read aloud, as long as time permits. Then, when the reader has ceased, the president makes an address and exhortation to the imitation of these good things. Then we stand up all together and send forth our prayers; and, as I before said, when we have ceased praying, bread and wine and water are brought, and the president utters both prayers and thanksgivings with all his might, and the people assent, saying Amen." "Those who are wealthy and ready to give, each according to his own pleasure gives what he pleases, and that which is collected is deposited with the president, and he gives assistance to the orphans and widows, and to those who are in want through any other cause, and to those who are in prison, or the stranger, and, in a word, there is care taken for all those who are in necessity." This description of the worship and the customs of the Christians, written not much more than one hundred years after the crucifixion of our Saviour, is full of the deepest interest. In the Apology from which it is taken every part of the Christian faith and practice is eloquently defended; and so great an impression did this writing of Justin's produce upon the Emperor Antoninus, that he gave commandment that none should henceforth be molested simply because they were Christians. In a letter which is preserved, and which was written either by Antoninus or by his successor M. Aurelius, a very remarkable testimony is borne to the Christians by the heathen Emperor. Speaking of the earthquakes which were occurring at that time, he says that the Christians are much more brave and confident in danger than their heathen fellow-subjects, and so favourably did he regard them, that he directed that the informers who should molest these innocent men should be made to suffer the punishments which they had tried to inflict upon the Christians.

After doing this good service to his religion by presenting this Apology to the Emperor, Justin left Rome and went into Asia Minor. At Ephesus he met with a Jew of great eminence and learning, who had fled from his country in the late war which Barchochab had carried on against the Romans. Since that time he had lived in Greece, and conversed much with the philosophers to improve his mind and knowledge. With this learned man Justin entered upon a discussion as to the truth of the Jewish and the Christian religion. For two days they argued the whole subject, and Justin has left us a long and minute account of their discussion. Every argument which Trypho the Jew could bring forward in favour of Judaism is met by Justin with the greatest skill and learning, and the truth of Christianity is clearly established.

And not only does Justin show that the Jews were utterly wrong in clinging to their law, which had now been superseded by the Gospel, but he also justly reproves and condemns them for the implacable spite and malice which they showed against the Christians. He says that they sent persons up and down the world to spread abroad that Jesus the Galilean was a deceiver and an impostor, and that His whole religion was nothing but a cheat; that in their public synagogues they solemnly anathematized all that turned Christians, hated them with a mortal hatred, oppressed and murdered them whenever they got them into their power.

The Jews were thus, as we find, continuing just in the same spirit in which they are described in the Acts of the Apostles.

After his dispute with the Jew Trypho at Ephesus, Justin soon left that city and returned to Rome, where he was quickly involved in contention with another great enemy of the pure faith of Christ. The heathen philosophers could tolerate with great calmness any forms of degrading superstitions which were brought into Rome from the various countries over which she had rule, but the pure religion of Christ exasperated and embittered them. That religion which condemns so utterly an unholy and licentious life, which was the life of most of the so-called philosophers, they desired to suppress, as a witness against themselves. With one of these men, named Crescens, dangerous from his influence, and from the extreme viciousness of his character, Justin now had frequent disputes. Crescens was what was called a *Cynic* philosopher, a man bound by his profession to despise pleasure, but he was a notorious profligate, false and cruel, and a constant and bitter foe of the Christians. Justin desired to have a public disputation with him in the presence of the Emperor, declaring that he could convict him of entire ignorance of the Christian religion which he denounced, and could rebut every charge which he made against the Christians. This, however, he could not obtain. The Emperor who had now succeeded to the throne was a bigoted supporter of the old Pagan religion, and not likely to treat the Christians with impartiality. Indeed, a flagrant instance soon happened at Rome of the grossest injustice towards them.

This, which was the occasion of the second Apology of Justin being written, is related by him in the beginning of that treatise as follows.

A woman at Rome had, together with her husband, lived in all manner of licentiousness, but being converted to Christianity, she sought by all arguments and persuasions to reclaim him from his loose and vicious life. The husband, however, still continued his old habits, and the wife at length, being unable to endure his conduct, procured a bill of divorce from him. Upon this the husband, enraged, denounced his wife to the Emperor as a Christian, but the wife putting in a petition for delay, and promising that afterwards she would answer the accusation, the husband could not proceed to punish her.

Upon this he turned his vengeance against Ptolomæus, who had been the means of converting the wife to Christianity, and procured an officer to cast him into prison on the bare charge of being a Christian. This was illegal, according to the proclamation of Antoninus, to which we have before referred; but in the case of the Christians the laws were continually violated. Not only did the officer keep Ptolomæus in prison for no offence but simply because he confessed himself a Christian, but Urbicus, the governor of the city, having him brought before him, actually condemned him to death on this ground. Upon this Lucius, a Christian who stood by, remonstrated with the governor on his injustice, and immediately he, together with a third Christian who joined with him, were condemned to death also. Justin resolved to address a remonstrance to the Emperor and to the Roman Senate. "I, for my part," he says, "expect that by some or other of these men I shall be seized and crucified, and especially do I expect this from that lover of noise and of boasting, Crescens."

But, though he knew well the danger which threatened him, this undaunted witness for the truth boldly defended the Christians, and denounced the injustice of persecuting them. We find him first examining two specious cavils with which the Christians were met. "Why," said the heathen, "if you are servants, as you say, of the God of heaven, do you not depart to your God and leave us unmolested?" To this Justin replied, that Christians owed a duty to the world and to their fellow-creatures in trying to improve and instruct mankind, and that they could not desert their post by committing self-slaughter. Again, the heathen objected, "Why, if it be true that you are servants of the Almighty, does He not protect you?" To this he replied by describing the fall and degradation of the race of man, and the power which evil spirits were permitted to exercise in the world. So far is it from the fact that God does not protect Christians, that it may be inferred that were it not for them a universal destruction would be sent upon the world. If now they are called upon to suffer, there is a future state in which abundant recompense will be given to them. The mischief created by the evil spirits is being removed and destroyed by the Incarnation of Christ, so that it is of the highest importance to the world that Christians who can use the powers which come to them from Christ should continue among men.

Having disposed of these cavils, Justin then argues strongly against the stoical philosophy, which was the more bold as M. Aurelius, the Emperor, was himself greatly devoted to this. Justin desired that this apology might be allowed to go forth to the world by the leave of the Senate, that all might judge fairly of the Christians. But this was not likely to be conceded in the then state of the Roman world. Crescens, the cynic, who had been thus publicly denounced by Justin, followed him up with revengeful hatred. He persuaded the Emperor that this bold Christian apologist was most dangerous to the cause of philosophy, and he at length induced him to order that Justin should be committed to prison. That which subsequently befell this holy man, and some companions who were apprehended with him, is told in an ancient history of his martyrdom, which, on account of its touching simplicity and deep interest, we shall give to the reader entire.

"Justin, Chariton, Charito,* Pæon and Liberianus, being apprehended, were brought before the governor of Rome, named Rusticus, and when they were placed before the tribunal, Rusticus said, 'Believe in the gods, and obey the Emperors.'

"*Justin.* There is no ground for blame or con-

* This is a woman's name.

demnation in our obeying the commands of our Saviour Jesus Christ.

"*Rusticus.* What form of philosophy dost thou profess?*

"*Justin.* I have applied myself to learn all forms of philosophy; but I have given in my adhesion to the teaching of the Christians, which is indeed true, though it pleases not those who are in error.

"*Rusticus.* Does that teaching satisfy thee, wretched one?

"*Justin.* Yes; since I follow it with right doctrine.

"*Rusticus.* Of what sort is that doctrine?

"*Justin.* It is that which teaches us to worship the God of the Christians, whom we hold to be the One original Maker and Creator of all things, visible and invisible, and our Lord Jesus Christ the Son of God, who was foretold by the prophets as about to come for the salvation of men, and a teacher of good instruction; and I, indeed, as a man, can speak but small things compared to His infinite divinity, for which a prophetical power is needed, since ancient predictions declared that He of whom I speak is the

* It will be remembered that Justin wore the dress of a philosopher.

Son of God, and I know of old time the prophets foretold of His coming among men.

"*Rusticus.* Where are ye in the habit of meeting?

"*Justin.* Where each one pleases and is able. Do you suppose that we all meet at the same place? Not so. The God of the Christians is not circumscribed by place, but being invisible He fills the heaven and the earth, and everywhere He is worshipped and glorified by the faithful.

"*Rusticus.* Tell me where you assemble, and into what place you bring together your disciples?

"*Justin.* I myself dwell above the house of a certain Martin, at the Timotine Bath, and during all the time of my two visits to Rome I have not known any other place of assembly than this. If anyone wished to come to me, I was ready to communicate to him the words of truth.

"*Rusticus.* Art thou not then a Christian?

"*Justin.* Yes, I am a Christian.

"*Rusticus* (*to Chariton*). Tell me, Chariton, art thou a Christian?

"*Chariton.* I am a Christian by the bidding of God.

"*Rusticus* (*to Charito*). What sayest thou, Charito?

"*Charito.* I am a Christian by the gift of God.

"*Rusticus* (*to Euelpistus*). What art thou?

"*Euelpistus,* the slave of Cæsar, answered: I too am a Christian, having been freed by Christ, and made partaker of the same hope by the mercy of Christ.

"*Rusticus* (*to Hierax*). And art thou a Christian?

"*Hierax.* Yes, I am a Christian, for I venerate and worship the same God.

"*Rusticus.* Justin has made you Christians?

"*Hierax.* I have long been a Christian, and I ever will be.

"*Pæon,* standing by, said: And I too am a Christian.

"*Rusticus.* Who taught thee?

"*Pæon.* From my parents I received this holy profession.

"*Euelpistus.* I always heard the words of Justin with pleasure, but from my parents I received my Christianity.

"*Rusticus.* Where are thy parents?

"*Euelpistus.* In Cappadocia.

"*Rusticus* (*to Hierax*). And where are thy parents?

"*Hierax.* My true father is Christ, and my mother is the faith in Him; but my earthly parents are dead. I was taken by force from Iconium in Phrygia, and brought hither.

"*Rusticus* (*to Liberianus*). What sayest thou? Art thou a Christian? Art not even thou pious towards the gods?

"*Liberianus.* I too am a Christian; I am indeed pious, and I worship the only true God.

"*Rusticus* (*to Justin*). Hear, thou who art accounted learned, and who thinkest that thou knowest the true teaching: if thou shouldest be scourged and then beheaded, art thou persuaded that thou shalt ascend into heaven?

"*Justin.* I trust that if I undergo these things I shall receive His gifts, for I know that for all who have thus lived there remains His merciful favour at the end of the world.

"*Rusticus.* Dost thou suppose, then, that thou shalt ascend into heaven to receive some recompense?

"*Justin.* I do not suppose it; I know it, and am confident of it.

"*Rusticus.* Let us come to business. Go ye altogether and sacrifice to the gods.

"*Justin.* No one in his senses falls into impiety from piety.

"*Rusticus.* If ye do not obey, ye shall be punished without pity.

"*Justin.* We pray constantly that, having been afflicted with punishment on account of our Lord Jesus Christ, we may obtain salvation; for this shall be to us a source of safety and of confidence before the dread universal judgment-seat of our Lord and Saviour.

"In the same manner all the martyrs said: 'Do what thou wilt; we are Christians, and we do not sacrifice to idols.'

"*Rusticus.* Let those who are not willing to sacrifice to the gods and to obey the decree of the Emperor be scourged and led away to be put to death, according to the law.

"Then the holy martyrs, glorifying God, were led out into the accustomed place, and their heads were cut off, and they perfected their testimony with the confession of the Saviour. But some of the faithful, taking away their bodies, secretly buried them in a fitting place, the grace of our Lord Jesus Christ working with them, to whom be glory for ever and ever. Amen."*

It is scarce possible to find, among all the re-

---

* The Acts of the Martyrdom of St. Justin and his Companions, printed in vol. ii. of St. Justin's works. (Ed. Otto.)

mains of Christian antiquity, any which in a more graphic and striking way puts before us what the holy martyrs of old had to suffer, than does this simple account. Exposed to the scorn, the contempt and derision, as well as to the cruel and unchecked violence of the heathen judges, constancy, wisdom, and a fearless courage were indeed needed by them. Slaves, accustomed to tremble at the rough words of their master, and women unused to take a public and prominent position, were suddenly called upon to defend their faith before the great and powerful, in the face of threatened torture and death. That, in spite of all, they bore such noble witness for the truth as St. Justin and his companions did, we must truly acknowledge to be a signal triumph of the all-powerful grace of God. The martyrdom of Justin took place in the year 165 A.D. As the earliest Christian writer of works of any length and controversial importance, he takes a very prominent position in Church history; and when we add to this the holy character of the man, and the noble witness which he bare in his death, we must needs regard him with the deepest interest and admiration.

ST. IRENÆUS.

St. Irenæus was probably born at Smyrna, or at some neighbouring place in Asia Minor; and in his early youth he had, as he tells us himself, the privilege of being instructed by Polycarp, the famous Bishop of Smyrna. From him he learned to look with dread and horror upon those false opinions upon our Lord's nature, and other important points of faith, which were unhappily so prevalent in the early Church; and from him too he learned that earnest and fervent zeal for the true religion which made him so valuable an instrument in the hands of God in spreading and maintaining the Gospel of Christ. It is probable that Irenæus accompanied St. Polycarp in the journey which he made to Rome to confer with Anicetus the Roman bishop, about the time for keeping Easter, and that at the instance of Anicetus he then determined to go into Gaul, in the south of which country there were at that time many Christians who spoke, as Irenæus did, the Greek language.

At this time Pothinus, who was also a Greek, was the Bishop of Lyons, the chief city of Celtic Gaul, situated at the confluence of the Rhone and the Saone—a city famous then, as it has been ever since, for its trade and manufactures. Besides this, Lyons was also famous for the splendour of its games and festivals, especially for one celebrated in memory of the Emperor Augustus Cæsar upon the first day of August, which was to prove a fatal day for many of the devout soldiers of Christ in that city.

Irenæus had been for several years labouring as a presbyter in the Church of Lyons, under the Bishop Pothinus, when, in the year 177, the same persecution, to which we have before alluded as having been begun by M. Aurelius the Emperor, fell heavily upon the Church in Gaul. Of the sufferings and constancy of the martyrs who were affected by it, we possess a detailed account, written probably by Irenæus himself, and which is so striking, that we shall give some part of it to the reader.

"Other historians," writes Eusebius, the Christian historian, who has recorded these things, "would care to hand down victories in wars, and trophies gained against enemies, and the mighty deeds of soldiers stained with blood and numberless slaughters, for the sake of exalting their children or their country; but the history which tells of our way of living shall record on imperishable pillars those most peaceful wars waged for the repose of the soul, and rather for the cause of truth than for country or those who are dearest. The bold stand of the soldiers of piety, and their much-enduring courage, the trophies raised against evil spirits, victories over unseen antagonists, and the crowns of triumph gained from such—these are what it shall record for everlasting memory.

"Gaul was the country in which those of whom I speak ran their race, of which land the most famous cities were Lyons and Vienne, past both of which the Rhone with its mighty stream flows. The Churches most famous in that land sent the account of their martyrs to the Churches of Asia and Phrygia, relating what had happened as follows:—' The servants of Christ who dwell in Vienne and Lyons in Gaul to the brethren in Asia and Phrygia, who have the same faith and hope of redemption as they, peace, grace, and glory from God the Father, and Jesus Christ our Lord. The full measure of our tribulation, and the extent of the rage of the heathen against the saints, and the endurance of the holy martyrs, we ourselves are not able to tell, nor indeed can it be expressed in writing; for the adversary pressed upon us with all his strength, giving first an earnest of that which his presence should afterwards effect, and then, going onwards, gradually trained and exercised his slaves against the servants of God, so that we were kept not only from the baths and the market, but were altogether prohibited from appearing anywhere in public. The grace of God contended against him and supported the weak, and ranged by their side firm pillars, who availed by their patience to draw the whole attack of the wicked one upon themselves. These, indeed, boldly contended with him, enduring every form of reproach and punishment, and thinking all this but little, were hastening to Christ, showing in reality that the 'sufferings of this present time are not worthy to be compared to the glory which shall be revealed in us.' * And first they nobly endured the attacks of the mob, their shoutings, their violent assaults, their hurling of stones, and all that a maddened people is wont to do to those it

* Rom. viii. 18.

hates. And then, when they were brought to the market-place by the magistrates, having been interrogated and made their confession before all the people, they were shut up in prison until the governor should come. . . Then indeed they were sifted and tried, and those who had most of the spirit of martyrdom were made manifest, for these with all readiness completed the confession of martyrdom. And there were also seen then those who were unready and unexercised, and still weak and unable to bear the effort of the great contest. About ten of these they put out from among us, who caused great grief to us, and injured the readiness of the rest who had not yet been apprehended, but who still, in spite of all they had to suffer, appeared with the martyrs, and did not desert them. All of us were terribly frightened by this uncertainty of confession, not fearing the punishments that were inflicted, but looking to the result, and dreading lest any should fall away. In place of those who had fallen day by day those of most worth were seized, so that all the zealous from both churches were gathered together, and all upon whom the Churches most depended. There were also arrested certain heathen servants of the Christians, as the governor had commanded publicly that all of us should be sought out, and these, by the craft of Satan, fearing the torments which they saw the saints suffering, and at the instigation of the soldiers, falsely accused us of feeding on human flesh and of various abominable crimes, which will not bear to be spoken of, and which it is hard to conceive that anyone could have been guilty of. Upon the report of these things getting abroad, all were savagely incensed against us, and even those who before were moderate then were greatly enraged; and that was fulfilled which was spoken by our Lord, that 'the time cometh when whosoever killeth you will think that he doeth God service.' Then, far beyond all expression, did the holy martyrs endure punishment, Satan eagerly striving that some blasphemous word should be spoken by their mouths. But beyond the rest, the fury of the mob and the governor and the soldiers lighted upon Sanctus, a deacon of Vienne, and Maturus, a new convert, but a noble champion, and Attalus, by birth a native of Pergamus, who had ever been the pillar and support of the Christians there, and upon Blandina, by whom Christ showed that the things which are little esteemed among men are with God thought worthy of much honour, on account of her love to Him, which was shown in power, and not boasted of in pretence. For when we all feared, and especially when her mistress after the flesh, who also was among the martyrs, was in great terror lest she would not be able to have courage for the confession, on account of the weakness of her body, Blandina was filled with such power that the successive bands of tormentors, who tortured her in every manner from morning till evening, were exhausted and overcome, so that they themselves acknowledged that they were foiled, and could do no more to her, but that they wondered at her being still alive—all her body being broken and torn, and any one form of the tortures used being sufficient to take away life, much more so great a number. She, the blessed maiden, like a noble combatant, seemed to gain fresh strength in her confession. To her the words 'I am a Christian, and among us nothing evil is done,' were continually a recovery and a refreshment and an ease from pain. Sanctus also, enduring all the tortures in a way extraordinary and superhuman, when the wicked ones hoped, through the continuance and greatness of the torments, to make him say something not fitting, contended against them with such firmness, that he would not even tell his name or nation or city, nor whether he were bond or free, but to all enquiries answered only in the Latin tongue, 'I am a Christian.' This to him was instead of a name, a city, a race, and was his reply to everything, and the heathen heard no other word from him. Eagerly did the governor and the torturers strive; and when at length they could do nothing more to him, at last they fastened on to the most tender parts of his body scales of brass heated red hot. His flesh indeed was burnt, but he remained without yielding, firm in his confession, being refreshed and strengthened by that water of life which cometh forth from Christ. His body was a witness of what had been done, being all wounds and sores, twisted and contracted, and having lost the very shape of a human being. For Christ suffering in him accomplished mighty glory, bringing the adversary to nought, and showing, for the example of the rest, that nothing is terrible where there is the love of the Father, nothing painful where there is the glory of Christ."*

The account tells further of numberless savage

* Eusebius, Hist. Eccles. v. 1.

cruelties practised against the unoffending Christians—their being exposed to wild beasts, to fierce dogs and furious bulls, their being kept in prison in their wounded state until they died, and then with fiendish malice their remains being burnt and the ashes thrown into the river, the heathen in their folly thinking that by this they could prevent that resurrection in which the Christians professed their belief. But the malice of the persecutors availed nothing, and the Christians nobly endured all the torments; and even those few who had at first been terrified into a denial of their faith, seeing the brave endurance of their brethren, again professed their religion, and were made to share with the others in the glories of martyrdom. Pothinus, the aged Bishop, with the weight of more than ninety years upon him, and a body so feeble that he could scarcely stand, nevertheless boldly professed Christ, and was put to death with torments. Blandina was again and again tried with the most excruciating torments, but nothing could move her constancy. It seemed as though all the malice of the executioners was not able to inflict death upon her, and she was almost the last victim who expired.

Of all this terrible outbreak of heathen cruelty Irenæus was witness, though he himself escaped. Of so great a multitude as the Christians in southern Gaul then were, it was impossible that all should be put to death; the more prominent were seized and punished, by way of terrifying the rest, and the weak and those most likely to be made to yield were also sought for, though, as in the case of the slave girl Blandina, in these the discomfiture of the persecutors was sometimes only the more signal. Irenæus escaped by God's providence, as there was work for him hereafter to do in the Church of God, but that he did not escape through any shrinking or cowardice is clearly proved by the fact that he was chosen by the surviving Christians to carry the letters giving account of the martyrs to the Bishop of Rome. In these letters Eleutherius, the Roman Bishop, was desired by the Christians of Lyons to receive him, not only as their brother and companion, but as a zealous professor and defender of the faith.

The Christians of Lyons soon gave a more distinct and certain proof of the estimation in which Irenæus was held even than this. They chose him to succeed their venerable martyred Bishop Pothinus, and in the year 179 he was consecrated to be Bishop of this Church which had been so ennobled by suffering. Great were the difficulties and dangers to the faith with which in this high position he had to contend. No sooner had persecution ceased, than the still more perilous trial of heresy came upon the Church. The opinions of the Gnostical teachers, Marcion, Valentinus, and Basilides, who entirely perverted every doctrine of the Christian religion, began to spread in Gaul, and to cause great danger to the faith. Irenæus is said to have summoned a general meeting of the bishops and presbyters of that country to protest against these mischievous errors. Anxiously desiring also to provide for the Church a permanent defence against such attacks, Irenæus composed a book " against heresies " of great value and importance. This book was written in Greek, but the greater part of the original has been lost, some portions only having been preserved by the Christian historians who have quoted it. Fortunately, however, an old Latin translation of the work exists, so that the valuable testimony of this early writer to the truth has not perished. What Irenæus tells us about the composition of the Holy Scriptures is very interesting. " Matthew produced his writing of the Gospel among the Hebrews and in their own language, while Peter and Paul were still preaching at Rome, and founding the Church. And after they had gone away (i.e. died), Mark, the disciple and interpreter of Peter, having himself written in a book those things which were preached by Peter, handed them down to us. And Luke, the follower of Paul, laid up in a book the Gospel preached by him. Then John, the disciple of the Lord, who also leaned upon His bosom, he too gave forth the Gospel while he was sojourning at Ephesus in Asia."* We have here distinct and unimpeachable testimony that the four Gospels are each due to an independent source, three of them to the testimony of members of the band of twelve Apostles, and St. Luke's to the witness of St. Paul, who, we are expressly told, had distinct revelations made to him by the Lord.† Written without consultation among the composers of them, in different countries, under different circumstances, and at different times, and yet exhibiting so wonderful an agreement in their testimony, the four Gospels give the most evident proofs of having been composed under the influence of the Holy Spirit of God.

* Eusebius, B. V. c. 8. † Gal. i. 12.

Besides what he says of the Gospels, Irenæus speaks of the Revelation of St. John, which he says was written at the end of the reign of Domitian, and of the epistles of St. John and St. Peter, from which he quotes passages. All these early testimonies to the prevalence of the Scriptures in the Church, and to their universal reception as having the authority of the Word of God, are very valuable. Irenæus wrote his book against heresies in the time of Eleutherius, Bishop of Rome. Eleutherius was succeeded by Victor, who with an unwise zeal again revived the dispute about the time of the celebration of Easter, and endeavoured to force the Churches in Asia Minor to yield to the Roman custom of celebrating it always on the Lord's Day, and not on the day of the Jewish passover. The Asiatic Churches naturally refused to yield to the Roman Bishop as he had no authority over them, and then Victor in his anger and pride proceeded to excommunicate them. This was an act of great mischief to the Church. Heresies and divisions were already too prevalent without this new cause of strife being added, and every quarrel and dissension among Christians was a fresh argument against them for the heathen to use.

Under these circumstances Irenæus, who, as

Eusebius says, was a peacemaker according to the meaning of the name which he bare, having called a meeting of thirteen bishops in Gaul, addressed in their name and his own a letter of remonstrance to Bishop Victor. He reminds him that there were many things in which Christians differed without thereby thinking it necessary to quarrel with one another; and that on this very point the venerable Polycarp and Anicetus, Victor's predecessor, differed, and were unable to come to any understanding, yet that they still continued in Christian love and fellowship together, and joined in the celebration of the Holy Communion. He earnestly exhorted Victor therefore to cultivate peace and charity.

And now, after a short cessation, persecution again broke forth upon the Church of God. Severus, the Emperor, at first favourable to the Christians, turned bitterly against them, and ordered punishments to be inflicted upon them in all parts of the empire. Especially, however, did he direct the persecution against the Church in Gaul; for in this province he had himself been governor, and he was well acquainted with the numbers and influence of the Christians there. Accordingly, a most bitter destruction now overtook the faithful Christians over whom Irenæus presided as bishop, and almost the whole of them were put to death. It is altogether most probable that Irenæus himself, as the most conspicuous and influential person in the Church, did not escape when so many perished, but as we have no authentic account of his martyrdom, it has been doubted by some whether he suffered. Others say that he was first tortured and then beheaded, and that so great a number of Christians perished in this persecution that the streets ran with blood. This was probably about the year 202 A.D., when the Emperor Severus published his ferocious decree against the Christians.

All that we read of Irenæus, as well as all his writings that have survived, lead us to look upon him as a man of a truly devout and Christian character. His zeal against heresy and error did not prevent him from taking a considerate and charitable view of those who differed from him in minor points, and his constant earnestness in watching over and instructing his charge in those times of terrible danger and rebuke, should make us cherish his name and memory with affectionate gratitude.

F

ST. CYPRIAN.

In the lives already recounted, we have had glimpses at the progress and trials of the Church in Asia Minor, Palestine, Italy, and France. We now turn to a different country, one in which flourishing Christian communities existed for many centuries, though now all is lost, barren, and infidel—the Roman province of Africa. This part of their dominions was of vast importance to the Roman Emperor and people. Its plains, fertile in corn, were the principal feeders of the large population of Rome. Here most of the great Roman families had possessions, and as deep an interest was felt at Rome as to what passed in Northern Africa as if it had taken place in Italy itself.

Owing to their intercourse with Rome, the Gospel soon reached Carthage and the province of Africa. In the latter half of the second century, Tertullian, a presbyter of Carthage, writes of the Church there as in a flourishing condition. He says, that the heathen complained "that Christianity was spreading in town and country, among all ranks, and even among the highest." A persecution of the Christians had already taken place in Africa before the time when Tertullian wrote.

About the end of the second century was born at Carthage the great man of whom we come now to speak, Thascius Cæcilius Cyprianus. He was born of a rich family, and well educated in all the instruction given to young men brought up in the religion of the heathen. He specially applied himself to the study of oratory, and became a teacher of this at Carthage. Gaining great fame and reputation, he lived in much pomp and plenty, in honour and power, his dress splendid, his attendants numerous, surrounded, whenever he went out, with a throng of followers. Up to the time when he was quite advanced in life, he continued in this condition, a believer, or, at any rate, a professor of belief, in the false gods of the Romans. His conversion to Christianity was due to the labours and persuasion of a presbyter named Cæcilius, whom afterwards he ever regarded with the most affectionate love, and whose name he took at his baptism.

No sooner was Cyprian baptized and admitted

into the Church than he applied himself with the utmost zeal to master all the doctrines of the Christian religion, and his great abilities and practised mind enabled him to make rapid progress. The Carthaginian Christians rejoiced greatly at having so illustrious a convert among them. Cyprian was ordained presbyter, but the people were not content with this, but, on the death of their Bishop Donatus, they eagerly demanded that he should be advanced to the highest dignity in the Church. From this Cyprian shrank; feeling doubtless that, as one so lately converted, he ought not to aspire to this great responsibility. But the people besieged his house and tried to compel him by force to yield to their wishes, and at length Cyprian consented, and in the year A.D. 248 was consecrated Bishop of Carthage. The beginning of Cyprian's rule as bishop was quiet and peaceable; but soon there broke out against the Christians a more bitter and terrible persecution than any which they had yet experienced. Decius, the Emperor, on reaching the throne, A.D. 249, declared openly that he purposed to *crush Christianity*. He ordered strict enquiry to be made about all persons suspected of not complying with the religion of the

State, and those who were found not ready to do so were to be compelled by tortures to yield. Should the tortures, after being often repeated, prove unavailing, they were to be punished with death.

At this time there had been no persecutions of the Christians for a long time, and many had joined the Church who were not earnest enough to give up all for Christ. These, when the threat of torture and the loss of all their earthly possessions was made, shrank in terror from their profession and sacrificed to the heathen gods. Many, however, firm in the faith, refused to do this, and perished at the hands of the heathen.

When the Emperor's edict came to Carthage, " Cyprian, Bishop of the Christians," was immediately proscribed by name, and his arrest was ordered. Upon this he had to consider anxiously what was fitting. On the one hand, it might be right to give an example to his flock, and by a brave testimony to confirm them in the faith; on the other, it might be of the highest importance that, during this time of trial and danger, when so many were falling, there should be a wise and prudent governor to watch over the Church. This last consideration prevailed with Cyprian, and he retired secretly from Carthage, not out of cowardice or from a desire to save his life, but from an earnest desire to do the best for his charge. "Immediately on the first approach of trouble," he says, "when the people with loud outcries constantly demanded my death, I retired for a time, not so much from care for my own life, as for the public tranquillity of the brethren, that the tumult which had begun might not be further excited by my presence, which was offensive to the heathen." "Therefore the Lord commanded us to yield and fly in case of persecution. He commanded this, and practised it Himself. For as the martyr's crown comes from the grace of God, and can only be received when the proper time is come, so he denies not the faith who, still remaining true to Christ, retires occasionally, but waits his time."

This was true Christian prudence. Thus also Cyprian writes to his clergy: "I pray you not to allow your prudence and care for the maintenance of tranquillity to fail; for although the brethren, in the spirit of love and charity, are desirous to visit those glorious confessors of the faith, whom the grace of God has rendered illustrious by such a glorious beginning, yet this must be done with precaution, and not in great numbers at a time, lest we provoke the jealousy of the heathen, and all access be forbidden, and so while we seek for much we lose everything. Take care also that due moderation be kept here for greater security, so that the individual priests who go to administer the Communion to the confessors, and the deacons who accompany them, may change according to some regular succession—because a change of persons will excite less jealousy; and in everything we must, gently and humbly, as becomes the servants of God, humour the times, and provide for the safety and tranquillity of the Church."

It may be that the motives which induced Cyprian to retire from danger and carefully and prudently to administer the affairs of the Church in his retirement, implied greater moral courage than presenting himself before the heathen tribunal as a candidate for martyrdom would have done. Many would be sure to accuse him of cowardice and slackness; but that he was led in what he did not by these but by far different motives his after conduct clearly showed.

During his retirement, Cyprian wrote no less than thirty-eight letters for the guidance and direction of the Church over which he presided, and these letters remain to us now to testify to his piety and wisdom. With one matter he was especially troubled. It has been already said that many at the first breaking out of persecution abjured their faith and lapsed into heathenism. These, having escaped the pressing danger, now desired very generally to return again into the Church, and were too readily and lightly received back by some of the presbyters of the Church. Very frequently the lapsed persons applied to those who had been confessors for the faith and had boldly borne the torture without yielding, to give them a recommendation, addressed to the clergy (called a *libellus*), requesting their restoration; and the clergy, out of respect for the martyrs, acted upon these *libelli*, and took back the lapsed persons without making them do penance. At this Cyprian was much displeased. That timidity and love of the world which had led the lapsed persons to yield, ought, in his judgment, to be treated as grave offences which needed to be repented of, and the sincerity of repentance ought to be tested by a certain prescribed form of Church penance. Accordingly he condemned the conduct both of the clergy and of the martyrs, in treating the lapsed with too great lenity.

Another mischief also followed from this mistaken kindness. Some of the more rigid disciplinarians, at the head of whom was Novatus, a presbyter of Carthage, offended at the laxity which prevailed, separated from the Church on this ground, and formed a sect. These men, who called themselves *Cathari,* or the *pure,* would not allow that in any case one who had lapsed ought to be received back into the Church, though they thought that, if sincerely penitent, he might find mercy hereafter. Cyprian opposed both these extremes, and insisted upon a middle course with great prudence and firmness.

In the meantime the Decian persecution continued to rage with still greater violence. The suffering Christians were scourged and beaten, and racked and roasted; their flesh was pulled off with burning pincers; they were beheaded, run through with swords, spoiled and plundered, chained and imprisoned, thrown to wild beasts, and burned at the stake. The persecutors sought to invent new species of torments, and with a desperate malignity kept their prisoners as long as possible from the death which they wished for as a release from their terrible trials.

In almost all cases the noble martyrs now stood firm, and astonished the heathen by their unconquerable fortitude. For two years did this fierce struggle continue, during all which time Cyprian remained in retirement. Now, however, a relief came, by the death of the cruel Emperor Decius, and Cyprian returned to Carthage, and set himself to reform the abuses which had sprung up in the Church during the time of persecution (A.D. 251). He immediately summoned a meeting of all the bishops in the neighbourhood of Carthage, and they agreed with him in deciding that the lapsed were to do penance according to the nature of the sinful compliance of which they had been guilty, while they also rejected the harsh views of Novatus, who would hold out to them no place of repentance.

The next year another Council met, which while it followed the same course, yet abridged somewhat the term of penance to be done, and made the restoration of those who had fallen somewhat easier. For now the Church dreaded the breaking out of another persecution, and they desired to be prepared for it by the strengthening and comforting of the weak. About this time there prevailed throughout the Roman world one of those terrible plagues which from time to time are sent upon mankind. At Carthage and in Africa vast multitudes perished; every house seemed to be visited; the streets were full of dead; and so great a panic seized the survivors that they ran away, leaving their nearest and dearest uncared for or unburied. The religion of the heathen taught them no better; but it was now to be seen that the pure religion of Christ led people to act very differently.

Cyprian called the Christians together, instructed them in the duties of mercy and charity, told them that their love was to extend, not only to their own people, but to the heathen also, and that they were to return the evil which had been inflicted upon them with good. And nobly were his words responded to. The Christians divided themselves into bands and went everywhere, succouring those that were smitten with the pestilence, whether heathen or Christian. They brought together all their property into a common fund, for the purpose of providing necessaries for those who were left destitute, and thus they nobly illustrated the spirit of the Gospel.

Yet the hard-hearted heathen attributed the pestilence to the anger of their gods at the Christians being allowed to live, and prepared again to persecute them. At the approach of this new persecution, Cyprian wrote a letter of exhortation to the North African Church of the Thibaritans, in which he thus expresses himself: "Let none of you, my brethren, when he sees how our people are driven away and scattered from fear of the persecution, disquiet himself, because he no longer sees the brethren together, nor hears the Bishop preach. We who dare not shed blood, but are ready to allow our blood to be shed, cannot at such a time be collected together. Wheresoever in those days any one of the brethren may be separated for a while by the necessities of the time, and absent in body not in spirit, let him not be agitated by the dreadfulness of that flight, and if he be obliged to retire and hide himself, let not the solitude of a desert place terrify him. He whom Christ accompanies in his flight is not alone; he is not alone who, preserving God's temple constantly, wheresoever he is, is not without God. And if in desert places, and on the mountains, a robber shall assault the fugitive, a wild beast attack him, or hunger, cold, and thirst destroy him, or if, when he passes over the sea in haste, the fury of the storm shall sink his vessel, yet Christ, in every place beholds His warrior fighting."

Thus did the good Bishop prepare them for persecution; but the storm, on account of political causes, did not immediately burst upon the Church in Africa. In the year 257, the Proconsul of Africa summoned Cyprian before him, and having required him to acknowledge the false gods of the Romans, and being steadfastly refused, he banished him to Curubis, a small city on the coast.

Soon afterwards many other Christians were either imprisoned or sent to work in the mines. At Curubis, Cyprian was most active in providing for the temporal and spiritual wants of these sufferers. While he sent large sums from his own revenues and from the Church chest for their support and for the relief of their distresses, he wrote thus to them: "In the mines the body is not refreshed by bed and couches, but by the refreshment and consolation of Christ. The limbs, weary through labour, lie upon the earth, but it is no punishment to lie there with Christ. Though the outward man be covered with filth, yet the inward man is the more purified by the Spirit of God. There is but little bread, but man lives not by bread alone, but by the word of God. There is but little clothing for the cold, but he who has put on Christ hath clothing and ornament enough. Even in this, my dearest brethren, your faith can receive no injury, that you are unable to celebrate the Communion. You do celebrate the most glorious communion; you do bring God the most costly offering; for the Scripture says, 'The sacrifice of God is a broken spirit; a contrite heart God doth not despise.'"

Thus did Cyprian keep up the Christian courage of his people as long as he was able. But the Roman Emperor, finding that banishing the bishops and clergy had the effect not of putting down Christianity, but rather, by forming new congregations, of increasing it, gave forth an edict in the year 258: "The bishops, priests, and deacons shall immediately be put to death by the sword, the senators and knights shall lose their dignities and property, and if after this they remain Christians, they shall suffer the same punishment of death. Women of condition, after confiscation of their property, shall be banished; the Christians in the service of the Imperial Court, especially slaves and freedmen, who have formerly made profession of Christianity or do so now, shall be considered as the property of the Emperor, and shall be distributed to labour in chains at the various public works."

The Emperor doubtless vainly supposed that by depriving the Christians of their clergy and rich men, he would be able to crush them. The execution of this cruel decree quickly lighted upon the devout and holy Bishop of Carthage. He was recalled from his banishment and summoned to Utica before the Proconsul, to receive his sentence.

But Cyprian was most anxious that his testimony for the truth should be given in Carthage, where he was so well known, and where he had so long governed the Church. Here his example would be most salutary, his last words fall on the most deeply interested ears. Accordingly, he concealed himself, and from the place of his retirement wrote his last letter to the Church: "I allowed myself to be persuaded to withdraw for a time, because it becomes the Bishop, in that place where he is set over the Church of the Lord to confess the Lord, that all the Church may be rendered glorious by the confession of their pastor. Let me in this retired spot await the return of the Proconsul to Carthage, to hear from him what the Emperors have commanded, in relation to the Christian bishops and laity, and to speak to him what the Lord in that hour wills that I should speak. But you, dearly beloved, keep peace and tranquillity in conformity with the discipline which you have always received at my hands, according to the commands of the Lord. Let no one of you bring the brethren into trouble, nor give himself up of his own accord to the heathen. Every man must then only speak when he is apprehended, for in that hour, the Lord, who dwells in us, speaks in us."

As soon as the Proconsul came to Carthage, Cyprian came to his own house and took up his residence there. Officers were immediately sent to apprehend him, and he was conducted to the Proconsul's palace, where, after having been some time kept waiting, at length he was brought before the Proconsul. He was then addressed: " Art thou Thascius Cyprian, who hast been Bishop and father to men of impious mind? The sacred Emperors command thee to do sacrifice.

Be well advised, and do not throw away thy life." The holy martyr replied: "I am Cyprian: I am a Christian, and I cannot sacrifice to the gods. Do as thou art commanded; as for me, in so just a cause there needs no consultation."

The Proconsul, angry at his boldness, upbraided him with all that he had done against (as he said) the interests of the Roman Empire, by encouraging and upholding the Christians. He then concluded by delivering his sentence: "I will that Thascius Cyprian be beheaded." To which the holy Bishop answered, "I heartily thank Almighty God, who is pleased to set me free from the chains of the body." He was then led away to a field where executions were performed, and himself laying aside his own clothes, and kneeling down composedly, he covered his eyes with his hand, and the executioner struck his head off, while the Christians pressed around him to gain some relic of his apparel, or sprinklings of his blood upon cloths. Thus perished a learned and eloquent, wise, prudent, and holy man. Great is his reward in heaven!

ST. ATHANASIUS.

THE LIFE of the great Christian Father whom we now come to consider introduces us to another and a very important portion of the Christian Church, and shows us a zealous and devoted Christian pastor boldly contending, not against the cruelty of heathen persecutors, but against the wicked arts and oppressions of nominal Christians. The persecutions of the heathen purified and elevated the Church, and by exhibiting the constancy of its martyrs, continually extended and enlarged it; but the heresies and scandals which arose within the Church itself were an unmixed evil, and led many souls for whom Christ died to destruction and perdition. In Alexandria, the capital city of Egypt, famous for its arts, learning, and commerce, the Gospel is said to have been first planted by St. Mark the Evangelist, and from him a line of chief bishops, or, as they were afterwards called, patriarchs, regularly descended.

From this Church the interior of Egypt and Ethiopia, or Abyssinia, received their Christianity, which, though clouded with ignorance and superstition, has remained down to the present day. The Church of Alexandria became very early famous for its learning, and for the subtle disputations on religious subjects which took place there. By these many of the learned and philosophical heathen were attracted to embrace the Gospel; but the spirit of free enquiry and discussion which was thus encouraged led to many false and vain opinions being spread abroad, which distracted the Church and brought reproach on the Christian name.

One of the opinions most mischievous to Christianity was that started early in the fourth century by Arius, a presbyter of Alexandria, who taught that our Saviour was only the highest and most divine of created beings, and not very God, of the same substance with the Father. This opinion attracted great numbers. It seemed to be more agreeable to human reason than the orthodox faith; and to those trained to rely upon their reason, as the Alexandrian Christians were, it was very seductive. But God raised up a notable champion for the true faith against these errors, who spent his life in combating them by preaching, writing, and discipline, and to whom we owe, under God, the preservation of the right doctrine of the Holy Trinity. Athanasius was born at Alexandria, about the year A.D. 296. Nothing is known as to his parents or family, but he doubtless gave good promise in his youth of what he afterwards became; for Alexander, the Archbishop of Alexandria, brought him up in his own family, and superintended his education with a view of educating him for the Christian ministry. At a suitable age he ordained him deacon, and Athanasius immediately began to give an earnest of his great talents and zeal by assisting his bishop in maintaining the true faith against Arius and his followers, who were now much increasing in Alexandria. Indeed, so rapidly were these opinions spreading—not only in Alexandria and Egypt, but throughout the Christian world —that Constantine, the Roman Emperor, a Christian, and one deeply interested in maintaining the true faith, thought it desirable to summon a general assembly of the Christian bishops and clergy, to take these things into their consideration. Accordingly, he issued his letters, inviting them to assemble at Nicæa in Bithynia, in the same province with Nicomedia, where he himself kept his court. Hither came together, in the year 325, about 300 bishops and a very large number of presbyters and deacons. Among the bishops was Alexander of Antioch, and among the deacons was the young Athanasius, full of zeal to support the true faith.

This Council, so famous in the history of the Church, met on June 19, A.D. 325, in the great hall of the palace at Nice. The Emperor Constantine treated the assembly of Christian bishops with the greatest courtesy and respect. He came into the Council, not attended by his guards, but by persons eminent for their faith and piety. Clothed in his most splendid robes, he sat down in the chair which had been prepared for him, and speaking in the Latin tongue, which by an interpreter was translated into Greek, told the bishops that he most earnestly desired the prosperity of the Church of God; that now that they were delivered from the persecutions of heathen tyrants, the greatest danger arose from their own divisions; and he prayed them heartily to do all that they could to restore unity and peace to the Church of God. The Council then proceeded to consider the opinions of Arius, which were read out of his own writings, and having almost unanimously condemned them, they drew up a confession of faith or creed, to which they subscribed, and which we still accept and reverence as the declaration of the right faith. Arius and his associates were condemned to be banished, and his books to be burned.

In all the discussions which took place at the Council, Athanasius bore a very prominent part, as the assistant of Alexander, the aged Bishop of Alexandria, to whom it more especially belonged to promote the cause against Arius. He began to be regarded as the most able champion of the orthodox faith; and when, soon after their return from the Council, Alexander died, Athanasius was chosen, by the special direction of the late venerable Archbishop, to fill his place. The people of Alexandria had vehemently demanded his consecration, and when they had obtained it showed every sign of joy and rejoicing. At this time he was only twenty-eight years of age, but so great was his reputation that his youth was not considered an impediment to his undertaking so high and responsible an office. He proceeded to show by his zealous discharge of the duties of a bishop that the choice had been a wise one. But great were the difficulties with which he had to contend.

About the year 331, the Arians, having persuaded the Emperor that they were ready to conform to the faith of the Church, were recalled from banishment, and Athanasius was directed to re-admit them into the offices which they had held in the Church. But the Bishop, knowing well that they were acting deceitfully, refused to obey, and at the same time wrote to the Emperor to justify his refusal, with which Constantine was satisfied. Failing in this, the Arians now sought to ruin Athanasius by inventing false charges against him. One of these charges was that Macarius, a priest, acting under the orders of Athanasius, had forcibly entered a church where a priest named Ischyras ministered, during the time of divine service; that he had overturned the communion table, broken one of the consecrated chalices, burned the sacred books, and utterly destroyed the church. Athanasius made his defence before the Emperor in person, and showed that Ischyras was not an ordained priest, and that hearing he was officiating, he had sent Macarius to enquire into it, who, finding Ischyras ill in bed, had merely left a message for him from the Bishop, requesting him to discontinue his irregular proceedings. But though Athanasius easily disproved this charge, it was again and again renewed against him; and he was also charged with the murder of a bishop named Arsenius, though in reply he produced the man said to be murdered alive and well. The Emperor was satisfied, but the enemies of Athanasius were yet able to procure his condemnation by a Council which met at Tyre, which took upon itself to depose and excommunicate him. Athanasius appealed to the Emperor, who ordered his accusers to meet him face to face in his presence. On this they abandoned their previous accusations, but artfully made a charge against him which the Emperor was more likely to regard as a serious crime. They accused him of trying to prevent the exportation of corn from Alexandria to Constantinople. Probably the good Bishop was taken by surprise at this strange charge, and not having evidence at hand to disprove it, Constantine was induced to think that it was true. Accordingly, he decreed the banishment of Athanasius from his see, and ordered him into Gaul. This sentence, however, did not amount to an actual decree of banishment, as the Emperor did not fill up the place of Athanasius in his see. Indeed, it may have been more out of regard to the Bishop than out of anger that he was told to leave Alexandria, and with the hope of healing the divisions which existed in the Church.* Athanasius retired to Trèves, where he was received with the greatest honour, while the people of Alexandria eagerly petitioned for his recall. In the year 337, Constantine died, and in the following year Athanasius was restored to his see by Constantine II., who had the highest respect and affection for him. The people and the clergy of Alexandria testified their joy at his return by the greatest rejoicings; but his unwearied enemies proceeded to bring charges against him to the Emperor Constantius,† who was at length induced to declare Athanasius deposed, and to appoint a successor. To meet this, the persecuted Bishop held a council at Alexandria, which declared all the charges made against him utterly unfounded. Julius, Bishop of Rome, was now called in as arbitrator by both parties, but the Arians refused to appear; and soon afterwards, the Emperor Constantius being

* Gibbon's Decline and Fall.
† He was joint emperor with Constantine II., and had Egypt as part of his dominions.

favourable to their cause, they held a council at Antioch, deposed Athanasius, and appointed Gregory of Cappadocia in his place. The orthodox Christians at Alexandria endeavoured to resist, but the governor of Egypt assailed them with cruel violence, and Athanasius was compelled to fly to Rome, where he was most honourably received by Julius, and acquitted of all the charges made against him in a Council held to try his cause. Another Council, held at Sardica, did the like, and sent delegates to Constantius to implore him to replace Athanasius in his see. Constantius now became favourable to him, and ordered his return, which was facilitated by the murder, about this time, of Gregory, the intruding bishop, under what circumstances it is not known. Once more did the great champion of the faith return to his see, amidst joy and welcome, and at once proceeded to take severe measures against the Arian faction. But the Archbishop was marked out by Providence for a series of trials such as perhaps no other man went through for so long a time. The fickle Constantius now gave ear to the Arians. Athanasius was proscribed, and his friends and supporters persecuted, and a third time he had to fly from his see, which was filled by an illiterate man of bad character, called George of Cappadocia. Cruel was the persecution which was now directed against the Christians who held the true faith in Egypt, and Athanasius himself would doubtless have been put to death could he have been found. But the monks and hermits, who now lived in great numbers in the deserts of Egypt, affectionately and watchfully protected him, and here in these solitudes Athanasius had leisure to compose some of his valuable works in defence of the true faith, while from his retirement he addressed a letter to his persecuted flock to comfort and strengthen them in their trials. In the year 361, Constantius, the great patron of the Arians, died. He was succeeded by Julian, commonly called the Apostate, who, at the commencement of his reign, ordered the restoration of the bishops banished by Constantius. This was rendered the easier in the case of Athanasius, inasmuch as George the Cappadocian was slain at that very juncture in a tumult raised by the heathen population of the city. Athanasius, on his return, behaved with great lenity and kindness towards those who had been his enemies, devoting all his energy and zeal to the restoration of order and the building up of the Church which had been so sorely tried. But now he was to encounter a new class of foes, who, taking advantage of the opinions of the reigning Emperor, proceeded to attack him. Julian had abjured Christianity and again adopted the old superstitions of the heathen religion, and on his accession all the heathen in his dominions, who were still numerous, showed signs of exultation and triumph. The Alexandrian heathen accused Athanasius to the Emperor of being a principal foe to their false gods—an accusation which was perfectly true, and in which the Bishop gloried. His banishment was ordered, but he retired this time without sorrow or pain ; and he predicted that his absence would not be a long one, as this foe to the Christian name would not be permitted to remain long in power. It turned out as he had predicted. Only for a few months had he to conceal himself in the monasteries, when Julian died, and Jovian, a zealous Christian, succeeded him in the throne. By Jovian, Athanasius was at once recalled, with every mark of honour and esteem. But his reign, unfortunately, was only a short one, and Valens succeeded, who was known to be, unhappily, inclined to the Arian heresy. However, for some years he left the orthodox bishops undisturbed; but in the year 367 he made a decree that all those bishops who had returned to their sees on the death of Constantius should again be banished. For the fifth time the weeping Christians of Alexandria saw their beloved Bishop driven forth; but when they perhaps thought in despair that he never would be allowed to remain among them to minister for their comfort and instruction, God mercifully changed their sorrow into joy. In a few months Athanasius was allowed to return, and from that time to the date of his death, 373, to remain unmolested, actively engaged in the labour of teaching and ministering to his people and defending the true faith by his writings. For forty-six years did he continue in his high office, and died in extreme old age, having fought an undaunted and persevering battle for truth through his whole life. No man was ever subject to more atrocious calumnies. Vice and immorality of every sort was imputed to him, but by God's help and his own unquailing firmness, he disproved and lived down every accusation, and died without a blot or stain upon his name. Gibbon, the infidel historian, to whom any earnest struggles for truth were usually a mere jest and a subject for contempt, is forced to acknowledge the grandeur of the heroic character of Athanasius, and to admit that " he displayed a superiority of character and abilities which would have qualified him, far better than the degenerate sons of Constantine, for the government of a great monarchy." By one who had the best opportunities for knowing his character, he is described as " humble in his mind as he was sublime in his life; a man of an inimitable virtue, and yet withal so courteous that any might address him; meek, gentle, compassionate, and amiable in his discourse, but much more so in his life; of an angelical look, but much more of an angelical temper and disposition; mild in his reproofs, and instructive in his commendations, in both which he observed such even measures, that his reproof spoke the kindness of a father, and his commendation the authority of a master, so that neither was his indulgence over tender nor his severity austere, but the one savoured of gentleness and moderation, the other of prudence, and both the effect of true wisdom and philosophy."* The name of Athanasius is perhaps most familiar to many of us by the Creed which is called after

* Gregory of Nazianzum.

him. But this was not written by him, but probably by Hilary, Bishop of Arles in France, about a century after the Council of Nice. As, however, it contains an explicit declaration of the doctrines for which Athanasius, amidst so many trials, contended, it is not unfittingly called by his name. Among the numerous writings which Athanasius left behind him, there was one which was especially esteemed in his day, and which had important effects, as it is said that mainly through this the great Augustine was converted to Christianity. The writing of which we speak was the Life of St. Anthony, a famous hermit of the deserts of Egypt, and who was almost the first Christian who practised what is called the ascetic life. Anthony had vast crowds of followers, who, as they multiplied, drew together in common establishment, and still keeping the name of monachi or monks (those who live alone) which they had at first received, came also to be called cenobites (those who live in common). In the miserable state of society which prevailed towards the close of the Western Empire, there was much to excuse men withdrawing into solitudes that they might practise devotion more uninterruptedly, but we cannot give to any of these recluses, however devout, the same sort of honour that we do to Athanasius, who laboured not for himself, but for his fellow-men—for the Church of God, that it might keep the deposit of the faith unimpaired, and that all the high hopes which are founded upon the perfect Godhead of our Divine Redeemer might not be frustrated.

> Great Athanasius! beaten by wild breath
>   Of calumny, of exile, and of wrong,
> Thou wert familiar grown with frowning death,
>   Looking him in the face all thy life long,
> Till thou and he were friends, and thou wert strong.
>
> The "eye of Alexandria," rais'd on high,
>   Unto all Christendom a beacon-light:
> Thou from our tossing waves and stormy sky
>   Art in thy peaceful haven hid from sight;
> But still thy name hath leave to guide us thro' the night.
>   (WILLIAMS' *Cathedral*.)

ST. HILARY.

THE NAME of Hilary, Bishop of Poitiers, in France, must be regarded with veneration by all those who love and honour the true faith in the doctrine of the Blessed Trinity, of which he was a defender, second in zeal only to Athanasius himself. The Latin hymn called the "Creed of St. Athanasius," which we use in our Church Service on certain holidays, has been proved almost to demonstration to have been composed by him,* and the sufferings which he endured at the hands of Emperors who favoured the false teaching of Arius commend him to our sympathy and respect. Some, indeed, of Hilary's writings breathe a bitter and fierce spirit, but he felt deeply the danger to the souls of Christians of error on the great doctrines of the faith, and this, perhaps, more than his own sufferings, provoked him occasionally to write more angrily than

* By Dr. Waterland, in his treatise on the "Athanasian Creed."

became a Christian teacher. But in his constancy and zeal, and in the devotion of his life to the cause of Christ, he was a bright example of the power of the Gospel. Easy would it have been for Hilary, by a pretended compliance with the Arian opinions prevalent in his time, or by not taking a marked and especial stand against them, to have purchased security, ease, and wealth; but this was not his view of a Christian bishop's duty. He considered himself pledged to "endure hardness as a good soldier of Jesus Christ," and to "earnestly contend for the faith which was once delivered to the Saints."

Hilary was born about the year 320, at Poitiers, a city famous in the early days of France. At this period the Christian religion had spread very generally through France, and was already beginning to gain the ascendant over the waning and dying forms of heathen superstition. The soil of France had been dyed by the blood of martyrs, and in that land had been shown some of the most wonderful examples of Christian courage and devotion. An abundant harvest had sprung from the seed thus sown, and many were attracted to the profession of Christianity by witnessing or hearing of its power as shown in the patient endurance of the martyrs.

At the time of Hilary's birth there were many Christians at Poitiers, but his family, which was one of high rank, had not yet been converted to the truth, and Hilary was born and educated as a heathen. It was not until he had grown to man's estate and was married, and the father of a young daughter, that any change in his opinions and belief took place. He himself has left it on record how this was brought about, and we find that it was with him as with St. Justin and some others of the Fathers: his conversion was produced by his own intelligent and candid study of the Scriptures, not by the persuasions or teaching of any one. In the first book of his treatise on " the Trinity," he speaks of the way by which he arrived at the knowledge of the truth. There was in him, he says, an ardent desire for knowledge, especially the knowledge of God. But when men would have him satisfy this by accepting the fables about the gods of the heathen, he saw how utterly unworthy of what his reason told him God must be, were these profane and foolish histories. Even by the light of nature he could perceive that God must be One—Eternal, Infinite, existing everywhere, knowing all things. In the study of the books of Moses he found these thoughts strengthened and cleared; the infinite greatness and the unity of God were demonstrated to him. From the knowledge thus gained of the Deity he was able to perceive that it could not be worthy of God to leave man, to whom He had given so much knowledge, to be annihilated for ever. To what purpose would this knowledge serve, if it only informed him of the certain and inevitable doom? Man must then be immortal; but what was to be his state in immortality? This reason could not teach him, neither could he find it clearly set forth in the books of the Old Testament. He went then to the Gospel, and there he learned of God becoming man to be the "way, the truth, and the life," of the Son of God "bringing life and immortality to light." Of the "Only-begotten Son who was in the bosom of the Father, revealing Him." He saw that by God becoming man the way was opened by which men might become the sons of God. The divinity and the humanity of Jesus seemed to him to satisfy all needs. In faith in the Gospel there was an abundant enlightenment of all the darkness which pressed upon the human spirit. The Gospel scheme for purifying, tending, and raising the spirit of man seemed to him all sufficient.

The teaching which Hilary thus found, coming, as it did, in his great need and darkness, was a treasure to him beyond all price. He eagerly embraced it, and was baptized as a Christian, together with his wife and his young daughter, Abra. He was willing now to submit his human reason in all points to the teaching of the divine revelation. He did not suppose that he could understand and fathom all things. He was content to accept mysteries as mysteries, but before all things to hold fast to the great revealed and declared truth that "the Word was made flesh." It was this spirit of humble faith which fitted Hilary especially for the great work which he had to do, and made him the undaunted and untiring defender of that which he had found of such priceless worth to his own soul.

A man of great natural ability and high culture, thus accepting the faith with all zeal and simplicity, could not but be highly prized by the Christian community of his native city; and accordingly we find that Hilary was soon chosen to be bishop of the Church in Poitiers. When consecrated to this office he felt himself pledged, as he tells us, to take care for the salvation of others. He began at once to preach against the errors of the Arians, which had spread all over the East, and were now beginning to corrupt the West. The soul-destroying heresy that Jesus Christ was an inferior being, not " of the same substance " with the Father, was everywhere the object of his attacks. He denounced it in his sermons from the pulpit, and he set himself to compose his famous treatise on " the Trinity," which he completed in twelve books. " This," says a learned writer, " is an excellent work. He has established the faith of the Church in a demonstrative manner. He has clearly detected the errors of the heretics, refuted them solidly, and answered all their objections clearly. It is the largest and most methodical work of any that we have in all antiquity on this subject."* For the faith which he thus earnestly advocated Hilary was soon to be called to suffer.

The governors of the Roman world were not indeed heathen now, as they had been at the beginning of this century, but they unhappily had been corrupted by the Arian perversion of Christianity, and were ready to enforce by punishments the false belief which they had adopted, just as the heathen emperors had

* Du Pin.

shown themselves eager to put down Christianity by violence. At this moment the Emperor of the whole vast dominions of Rome was Constantius. This prince had been guilty both of cruelty and treacherous dealing in his pursuit of power, and he did not show a more righteous spirit in matters connected with the Church. He acted completely in the interest of the busy faction of the Arians, and being at Arles in France, in the year 353, he caused a synod of the clergy to be summoned there, who, under his influence, condemned the doctrine of Athanasius and decreed in favour of Arianism. A similar synod was held at Milan in the following year, the Emperor having removed to that place, and a like declaration in favour of Arianism was made. The whole West seemed in danger of becoming Arian, as the East had already become, and it was, under God, due to the spirit and resolution of Hilary that this did not take place. The Emperor, having thrown all his influence on the Arian side, the governors of the provinces and the inferior officers eagerly imitated him, and the orthodox Christians were everywhere persecuted and ill-treated.

It was now that Hilary addressed a bold

and plain-spoken, but respectful, remonstrance to the Emperor. He called upon him to restrain his officers from proceeding with fury and violence against innocent persons, and from calling before them bishops and clergy, and pretending to judge of their doctrines, and if they did not consider them of the right stamp, sending them into banishment. He desired that the people might be allowed to enjoy the teaching of their own ministers, and to offer up their united prayers for the Emperor's happiness and safety. The orthodox faith, he said, was old, and dated back to Christ Himself, but Arianism was a modern religion, a thing of yesterday, and it was indeed tyranny to punish with chains and prisons, with whips and gibbets, those who refused to give up the ancient faith for these new views.

Doubtless this free and bold remonstrance would have speedily brought down upon Hilary the same punishments which the others whose cause he pleaded had to bear, but that it happened at this moment that there was great danger in France of invasion by the northern tribes of barbarians, and the Emperor was desirous of uniting all who favoured the Roman sway together to resist these enemies. Accordingly he not only tolerated Hilary's remonstrance, but even published an edict forbidding civil governors to try bishops in matters of doctrine. Having effected this with the civil power, Hilary next addressed himself to the bishops, who still professed the orthodox faith, and induced them to agree to refuse to hold communion with the chief leaders of the Arian party, among whom Saturninus, Bishop of Arles, was the most prominent. Saturninus immediately applied to the Emperor, and obtained leave to hold a synod at Beziers, near Arles, where he hoped to crush the orthodox party. Hilary met him at the synod, and producing a vigorous indictment, which he had drawn up against the Arians, endeavoured to read it there. This, however, he was not permitted to do. The bishops who favoured the right faith were overawed, and afraid of the Emperor's displeasure. Hilary found himself deserted by all save Rhodanius, Bishop of Tholouse, and he, though faithful to the right belief, was a man of no resolution, but was only supported by the courage of Hilary. Saturninus, seeing now an opportunity of crushing his adversary, obtained from the Emperor an order for his banishment, and Hilary accordingly was exiled into Phrygia, where he remained some years.

But though violently separated from the Church which was his especial charge, and having to contend with poverty and suffering, Hilary still laboured earnestly to uphold the true faith. It was now that he finished his great work "On the Trinity," and he also employed himself in writing letters to his friends in France, encouraging them to hold fast to the truth, and giving them information as to the designs of the Arians.

As it was reported that synods were to be held both in the East and West, in which the Arians would make an attempt to get their tenets affirmed, Hilary now drew up a treatise "On Synods," giving an account of the confessions of faith which had of late years been passed in the Eastern parts. In this he translates out of Greek the acts of the great Council of Nice, and explains the Greek terms which were much in use in the controversy, strongly insisting that the same language which had been employed by the Council of Nice should still be carefully adhered to.

Hilary had now been more than three years in banishment when a Council being held at Seleucia, in Isauria, he was summoned to it along with the other bishops, and a safe-conduct was given to

ST. HILARY AND FLORENTINA.—*Page* 123.

him. He relates that on his way to attend this Council a strange occurrence happened to him. As he passed a certain garrison, he went on the Lord's day into the temple there, when, immediately, a heathen maiden called Florentia, breaking through the crowd, cried aloud that a servant of God was come amongst them, and fell down at his feet, earnestly desiring that she might be signed with the sign of the cross. Her example was followed by her father Florentius, and he, together with his whole family, was baptized into the Christian faith. The new convert Florentia was animated with such zeal and love towards her spiritual father, that she insisted on following him in all his travels, and afterwards accompanied him back to Poitiers.

Arrived at Seleucia, Hilary found that the bishops were unwilling to receive him at the Council on the ground that he, as well as the other bishops of France, was tainted with Sabellianism, which maintains Father, Son, and Holy Ghost, to be but three several names of the same Person. Having cleared himself and the bishops of France from this charge, and shown that they held simply to the Nicene Creed, Hilary was admitted to the Council. But he soon found that there were very few indeed who held with him to the orthodox faith set forth at Nice. The great controversy in the Council was between those who held that the Son was of *similar substance* to the Father (Homoiousians) and those who maintained that He was not of similar substance (Anomoians). The opinions of these latter were rejected by the Council, which was however far from affirming the true Christian faith, of the Son being of the *same substance.*

At the conclusion of the Council certain deputies were dispatched to Constantinople to inform the Emperor of the result, and with these went Hilary, who was determined to make a vigorous effort to press the truth upon the Emperor himself. Accordingly, when arrived at Constantinople he used great endeavours to get an audience from the Emperor, and to be allowed in his presence to dispute against those who maintained the Arian views. He addressed to Constantius a document, in which he vindicated his own innocency against the accusations of his enemies, complained of the unhappy state of religion at that time, and of the constant multiplication of new creeds; and that men's minds were in a confused and excited state—that each put forward what he himself fancied as the true religion, and condemned all who differed from him with anathemas and threats. But the earnest entreaties of Hilary to be heard, and his forcible declarations of the evils which Christianity was suffering from the wranglings of the heretics, availed little. The Emperor was firmly bent on upholding the Arian views, and would not listen to Hilary. Still the zeal, earnestness, and perseverance of this undaunted champion of the faith, were a danger to the Arian party. If he were allowed to remain at Constantinople, he might at length succeed in getting heard against them, and at any rate his presence there gave support and courage to any in the city who still professed the right belief. They, therefore, procured an order from the Emperor that Hilary should return into France.

Ready as he was to revisit again his own charge and his native city, Hilary still had the affairs of the Universal Church so much at heart, that he stopped on his way at all those places where it seemed that his exhortations and preaching might be likely to do good. While thus employed in Italy, he was joined by Eusebius of Vercellæ, who was also returning from banishment, and who readily assisted Hilary in his work. Meantime the faithful in his French diocese, knowing that he was returning to them, were eagerly expecting his arrival.

There was one among them whose name became afterwards very famous in Church history, and who was so earnestly bent on seeing again his spiritual father, that he set out to Rome to meet him. This was Martin, afterwards the famous Bishop of Tours. He was a person of good family, and from his childhood brought up in the camp, his father being an officer in the Roman army. At ten years of age Martin had gone secretly to the Christian Church and had desired to be placed under instruction. After being a catechumen for eight years he was baptized, but still continued his military life until he obtained a regular dismissal from the general. Then going to Poitiers, to Hilary, he placed himself under his instruction, and became greatly attached to him. Hilary wished to ordain him deacon, but from this Martin shrank as holding himself unworthy, and would only consent to be admitted to the lowest degree of orders, that of exorcist. Martin had had to suffer persecution for his attachment to the right faith during the banishment of Hilary, and eagerly did he desire to meet again one who had with so much constancy defended the truth.

Just about the time when Hilary returned to his diocese, Constantius died, and was succeeded by Julian, who is generally termed the Apostate; because, having once been a Christian, he had renounced the faith and turned to heathenism. But though a heathen and afterwards a persecutor, Julian had no special affection for the Arians more than for the orthodox, and consequently, at the beginning of his reign, all the orthodox who were in banishment were allowed to return. The entrance of Hilary into Poitiers was a kind of triumph. Everywhere were seen marks of the most unbounded joy. The people had remained faithful to his teaching, and nothing did they so eagerly desire as again to hear his voice. His instruction was now once more zealously given to them, but beyond and besides his own diocese, Hilary felt that he owed a duty to the whole Church of France, as being confessedly the most influential bishop at that time in the land, and as having written most and suffered most for the faith. Everywhere the greatest confusion and distrust of one another had been produced by the spread of Arianism, and by the many synods and confessions of faith by which the Arians had tried to support their views. Some of those who had remained orthodox were for altogether excommunicating and separating from any who had made compliances to the prevailing heresy, but Hilary counselled a milder and a wiser course. There had been many mistakes, many surprises, and not a few would have been thus excluded from the Church who really desired to be orthodox, and were deeply sorry now that they were better informed for having weakly yielded to support Arian sentiments. Influenced by these views, the orthodox bishops of France held out the right hand of fellowship to all of their brethren who were ready to quit their errors and profess the truth.

At a synod held at Paris, certain of the most prominent Arian leaders were excommunicated, but the rest, at their own desire, were reconciled and received into communion. It would have been well for Hilary's fame if the mild and tolerant spirit which governed him on this occasion had always predominated in his dealings with those whose errors he justly condemned. But there remains on record a tract of his against the Emperor Constantius, written probably just about the time of that Emperor's death, in which he denounces him in language so bitter and vehement, that all his biographers have felt themselves obliged to protest against it. He calls Constantius Anti-Christ, and brands him as an abominable tyrant; as worse than Nero, than Decius, or Diocletian, who had been the great persecutors of old. He exhausts the language of invective against him, and declares that the Church had, under him, suffered more oppressions, more miseries, and more losses, than under any of the heathen emperors.

But if the zeal of Hilary in writing thus overpowered the moderation and charity which befitted a Christian bishop, it must be remembered that no greater trial could be endured by one whose whole soul was filled by the love of the truth, than to see the heritage of God made a prey by wolves; the simple and untaught Christians everywhere perverted, through their forcible separation from the faithful pastors who had guided them aright, and these pastors cruelly treated and thrown into prison, or driven to banishment, while men of ungodly lives and blasphemous opinions usurped their places and oppressed them with impunity. That Hilary fully realised a direct personal responsibility for every part of the Church where his influence could in any way be brought to bear, is apparent by that which is recorded as the last important action of his life.

In the year 364, when Valentinian was Emperor, Auxentius, who was well known as a favourer of Arian opinions, and who had been deposed and excommunicated by the orthodox bishops, prevailed with the Emperor to restore him to his bishopric of Milan, though it does not appear that he had really abandoned his false tenets. Hilary, believing that the Emperor had been deceived, at once hurried off to Milan, where the Emperor then kept his court, and denounced Auxentius as an Arian. Valentinian, who favoured the orthodox belief, called upon Auxentius to clear himself of this charge, and appointed some of the great officers of his palace, assisted by ten bishops, to conduct the trial, in which Hilary was the accuser. But the simple-minded honesty of Hilary was no match for the unscrupulous craftiness of the man whom he denounced. Auxentius, finding himself obliged to answer, and knowing that if he professed his real belief he should incur the censure of the Emperor, boldly declared that he believed Christ to be the true God, and to be of the same substance with the Father. He thus placed Hilary in the apparent position of a false accuser, although there is but little doubt that the falsehood was on the side of Auxentius, and the zealous Bishop of Poitiers had to quit the Emperor's court with somewhat of a stigma attaching to him, although his conscience told him that he had only acted with a single eye to the truth. On his return to his diocese, Hilary devoted himself with unremitting labour to his episcopal duties, and after a few years thus spent, died tranquilly at Poitiers, A.D. 369.

" He was a man," says Dr. Cave, " of more than common severity of life. In all the passages thereof, and indeed in all his writings, there breathes an extraordinary vein of piety ; he solemnly appeals to God that he looked upon this as the great work and business of his life, to employ all his faculties of speaking, of reason and understanding, to declare God to the world, and either to inform the ignorant or reduce the erroneous. He had a great veneration for truth, in the search whereof he refused no pains or study, and in the pursuit of it was actuated by a mighty zeal, and in the defence of it used a freedom and liberty of speech that sometimes transported him beyond the bounds of decency; his hearty concernment for religion meeting with the vigour and frankness of his temper, the natural genius of his country made him sometimes forget that reverence which was due to superiors, though otherwise he was of a very sweet, gentle temper. No considerations, either of hope or fear, could bias him one hair's breadth from the rule of the Catholic faith; he underwent banishment with as unconcerned a mind as another man takes a journey of pleasure; he was not moved with the tediousness of his journeys, the hardness of his exile, or the barbarity of the country whither he went; he knew he had to do with potent and malicious enemies, and that were wont to imbrue their hands in blood, but he carried his life in his hand, and dared at any time to look death in the face. He tells us that could he have been content to satisfy and betray the truth, he might have enjoyed his peace and pleasure, the favour and friendship of the Emperor, places of power and grandeur in the Church, and have flowed in all the pomps and advantages of secular greatness. But he had a soul elevated above the offers of this world, and truth was infinitely dearer to him than liberty or life itself. He was actuated by a true spirit of martyrdom, and seems to have desired nothing more than that he might have sealed his faith and his religion with his blood."*

Assuredly all those whose hopes are built upon that faith which Hilary, as God's instrument, did so much to uphold and preserve, must revere the memory of this holy and energetic champion of the truth.

* Life of St. Hilary ('Lives of the Fathers').

ST. BASIL.

In the Acts of the Apostles, on the occasion of St. Peter's Pentecostal Sermon, we read that there were strangers sojourning at Jerusalem from Pontus and Cappadocia.* It is most probable that, of these, some at least were among the number of the three thousand who were converted by St. Peter's inspired discourse, and by the great miracles of that day, and that these, when they returned to their own land, would not forget what they had seen and heard, but would be the planters of a Christian Church in those provinces of the Roman empire. Certainly Christianity was flourishing at an early date in Cappadocia, and the family which afterwards produced Saint Basil was, at a time long before his birth, famous for its devoted attachment to the true religion, and for the sufferings which it had to endure in the persecutions of the heathen emperors. His ancestors were also of the highest

* Acts ii. 9.

rank and greatest distinction. Both his father and his mother were remarkable for their gifts, both personal and mental, and his grandmother Macrina was a woman of the most devoted piety, who had been educated under St. Gregory, called " The Wonder-worker," Bishop of Cæsarea, and had suffered for the faith in the times of persecution.

It was under these favourable auspices that Basil was born at Cæsarea, in Cappadocia, in the year 329, A.D. His early education was chiefly conducted by his grandmother Macrina, but he was still young when his parents thought it expedient that he should leave Cæsarea, and travel to those places where the best teaching of all different kinds was to be found. When books were not in existence, teaching by word of mouth by famous doctors became an absolute necessity for those who desired to acquire learning; and to get this it was necessary to go from place to place, wherever the best professors were delivering their lectures. It was on this ground that the young Basil now left his native city, and travelling southwards, across the mountains of Cilicia, and passing at no great distance from Tarsus, the birth-place of St. Paul, came to the famous city of Antioch, where the best instruction was to be procured.

Of the important part which was played by Antioch in the early history of Christianity both the Holy Scriptures and all early writers tell us. Christianity was the prevalent religion there at the time of the arrival of Basil, but still the teacher under whom he placed himself for instruction in rhetoric was not a Christian but a heathen. His name was Libanius, and he was the most famous philosopher and orator of his age; but his highest honour, perhaps, is that he was the instructor both of St. Basil and of St. Chrysostom, the two greatest writers among the Greek Fathers of the Church. Libanius himself has borne testimony to the excellent character of Basil, and to the wonderful advances which he made in learning, while under his direction. Having obtained the particular instruction which he sought at Antioch, Basil now passed to Cæsarea, in Palestine, to obtain training of a different character. His career here is sketched by his friend Gregory of Nazianzum, who devoted one of his orations to the praises of Basil. "He went to Cæsarea to take part in the instruction given in that illustrious city, the metropolis in literature and learning. Let those speak of Basil who had the instruction of him, and who themselves gathered fruit from his learning; let them say how great he was to his masters, how great to his equals, being on a level with the one, and far surpassing the others in all kinds of learning; let them tell how much glory he obtained in a short time both among the people and among the chief men of the State, showing a fuller erudition than that age could comprehend, and a firmness and gravity greater even than his erudition—an orator among orators, a philosopher among philosophers, and, that which is the highest, a priest among Christians, even before he had entered the priesthood."

But though Basil had profited so remarkably by his studies, he was not satisfied until he had also gone through a course of teaching in the famous city of Athens, which might be described, far more correctly than Cæsarea, as the metropolis in learning of the ancient world. For many hundred years had Athens borne this character. It was the place where all the keen spirits of the world met to exercise their wit in discussions with one another, and to set forth any plausible or ingenious schemes of philosophy which they might have devised; for, to use the language in which the dwellers at Athens were described on the occasion of St. Paul's visit to that city, "All the Athenians and strangers which were there spent their time in nothing else, but either to tell or to hear some new thing."* To me, says Gregory of Nazianzum, Athens was indeed a golden spot, since it conferred upon me that great treasure, the friendship of Basil. They had been known a little to one another in their early years, being natives of the same country, and now they were brought together at Athens, Gregory being already a student of some standing there when Basil came.

The fame of Basil's acquirements had preceded him, and was so great, that Gregory was able to induce his fellow-students to forego, in Basil's case, those troublesome ceremonies of initiation which they were wont to practise towards all new comers. These rough practical jokes Gregory thought would ill suit the gravity and sober character of Basil, and his having saved him from them was the first act of kindness on Gregory's part which awakened the sense of gratitude in Basil. Other acts soon followed,

* Acts xvii. 21.

and the picture drawn by Gregory of the hearty Christian friendship in which these two young men lived, is one of the most beautiful records of Christian antiquity. " We mutually acknowledged our great affection one for the other, and the object of our pursuit being the same—namely, the true Philosophy—we became all in all to each other, living in the same house, eating together, having the same tastes, the same objects, ever increasing and strengthening our mutual love day by day. How shall I speak of these things without tears? We were both animated by an equal hope of acquiring learning, which is of all things the most likely to produce envy, yet there was no envy between us, but our contention was not which of us could get the first place, but which should yield it to the other, for both of us held the other's glory as his own. There seemed between us but one soul in two bodies."

By their friendship for one another and their devotion to the Christian religion, Gregory and Basil were saved from the dangers to religion and morality with which Athens abounded, and these two attracting other young men to them, gradually became the leaders of a sort of brotherhood, the fame of which spread everywhere.

At length came the time when Basil considered that his work at Athens was finished. He parted from all his friends with deep regret, but especially did he grieve to leave his beloved Gregory, even for a short time, as the two looked forward to a speedy re-union in Cappadocia.

But though so much time had been devoted to his studies at various head-quarters of instruction, Basil was not even yet satisfied. He now again seems to have repaired to Antioch, to put himself a second time under the great Libanius, and having perfected himself in oratory, he began to practise as a public pleader in the law courts at Antioch. But law did not satisfy him, and he applied himself in place of it to a very careful and earnest study of the Holy Scriptures.

He now left Antioch, and, passing southward, went into Egypt, where Christianity had perhaps taken a stronger hold at that time than in any other land. In Egypt he became known to that famous champion of the faith, Athanasius, Bishop of Alexandria, and he also was much interested in travelling about among the monks and hermits, who abounded everywhere in the more desert and wild parts of the country. These, as has been mentioned in the life of Athanasius, were often men of the most ardent devotion to religion, and in those troublous and unsettled times may be excused for leaving the society of their fellows and leading a comparatively useless life. Their strict and self-denying manner of living, their constant prayers and devotions, greatly struck St. Basil, and he afterwards introduced from their pattern the monastic state into Cappadocia.

Having now completed his travels, and acquired an admirable provision of all sorts of learning, Basil returned to his native place, Cæsarea in Cappadocia. He was anxious to carry out at once the way of life which he had so much admired in Egypt, and to live in solitude, occupied entirely with Christian studies. But his reputation was so great, that he found this almost impossible.

The Emperor Julian, who had apostatized from Christianity, and was vigorously trying to set up heathenism again, had known Basil intimately when a fellow-student with himself at Athens, and having the highest opinion of his power, was anxious to get him to his court to assist him in the government. This temptation Basil nobly refused, and so plainly did he write to the Emperor and reproach him for his conduct in having abandoned the faith of Christ, that Julian's favour was turned into anger. He inflicted a heavy fine on Basil, and it is probable would have even put him to death, had not he himself been suddenly removed to his account.

The Church felt a great relief when it knew that the heathen monarch was to be succeeded by a Christian, but the relief was not a real one; for Valens, the new emperor, was a favourer of the Arians, and the Orthodox Church was not likely to receive anything from him but ill-treatment and persecution.

Basil, who had been living for some years in a sort of monastic retirement among the mountains of Pontus, whenever he was able to do so, was now brought into a more prominent position. He had already been ordained deacon by the Bishop of Antioch, but he had shrunk from receiving priest's orders from Dianius, Bishop of Cæsarea, inasmuch as that prelate was tainted with Arian opinions. Now, however (362), Dianius, on his death-bed, sent for him, and confessing that he had been misled about the Arian creeds, desired reconciliation. On the death of Dianius a strange transaction took place as to the choice of his successor. The people of Cæsarea, in a violent and tumultuous manner, chose Eusebius, a man of virtue and authority, but a layman, and even an unbaptized person, though a professor of Christianity. They compelled some bishops, who were met to consult about the election, to baptize him, and to consecrate him as bishop. These sort of hasty and tumultuary ordinations were not uncommon in the early days of the Church, and may be explained by the excited state in which the danger of persecution caused the Christians to live, and the intense interest with which all regarded the matter of the government of the Church.

Eusebius, thus hastily and uncanonically promoted, made by no means a bad bishop, though he was deficient in ecclesiastical learning, as might be expected. St. Gregory, the devoted friend of Basil, acknowledges that he was a man of admirable piety and courage, although he laments that he acted unjustly towards Basil. Basil had been ordained priest by Eusebius soon after his consecration, but there had arisen an ill-feeling between them, due perhaps to the great estimation in which Basil was held, which may have excited the jealousy of the new bishop. However that may be, Eusebius, after having ordained Basil, prevented him from exercising his office, and Basil was strongly pressed by a great number of his admirers to separate from the communion of the bishop, on the ground of the irregularity of his consecration, and to set up a rival Church. From this, which would have been an act of unjustifiable schism, Basil, as might be expected, altogether recoiled, and under the circumstances he judged it most prudent to retire again from Cæsarea to his hermitage in Pontus, where, in addition to the solitude and repose which he desired, he soon had also the consolation of the society of his beloved friend, Gregory of Nazianzum.

Before Gregory, however, went to join Basil, some very interesting letters passed between the two friends, which give us great insight into their characters, and into the tender love which existed between them. Basil, full of eager enthusiasm, writes to Gregory the most glowing descriptions of the beauty and charms of his retreat. It was a high mountain, clothed with a thick shady wood, and watered on the north by cool and crystal springs, that issued from it. At the foot of the hill was a fruitful and verdant valley, through which a river forced its way over precipices of rock. The view from this mountain cave was charming, nor were there wanting other delights in this choice abode. The river abounded in fish, and the neighbouring hills in game; everywhere the music of singing birds charmed the ear, and a vast variety of flowers, spread over the valleys and plains, pleased the eye. Here were no beasts of prey, nor any inroads of men with their quarrels and perplexities, but all was peace and repose.

Gregory replied to this glowing description in a most amusing letter, in which he pleasantly ridicules his friend's enthusiasm; at the same time he was most eager himself to join him, and soon afterwards did so. Nor was Gregory the only one who came to join Basil. Great numbers gradually flocked to these solitudes, being desirous to practise their religion in peace and quietude under the direction of one so famous for learning and virtue.

Basil thus saw growing round him a society similar to those which he had visited in Egypt. The members of it employed themselves partly in religious worship and study. In order to guide them in passing their time to the best advantage, and to ensure regularity of life, Basil, in conjunction with Gregory, drew up a code of rules for these bands of hermits. This became afterwards the rule for all Eastern monasteries, and is still piously observed in hundreds of these establishments. However much one is tempted to resent this tendency among the early Christians to withdraw themselves by a cowardly shrinking from their proper place and duties in the world, yet it is impossible not to admire Basil and Gregory in their hermit life, so high and noble were their objects, and so devoted was their study of Scripture. Neither did Basil regard himself, as the more modern monks do, as entirely severed from the world, and as having no longer any interests therein. On the contrary, he would seem to have used his religious retreat for the purpose of enabling him to do his work in the world more effectually. This he plainly declared to his friends at Cæsarea who reproached him for having deserted them. He addressed them a letter of apology, explaining the value of his retirement, and cautioning them earnestly against the dangers to their faith which were abroad in the prevalence of the Arian opinions.

But for a man so distinguished as Basil, retirement, however much he might value it, was not possible for a long period. The episcopal see of

Neocæsarea, in Pontus, becoming vacant, the people eagerly desired to have Basil for their bishop, and a party who were opposed to his election endeavoured to prevent it by urging various charges against him. They accused him of false teaching, of innovations in religion—of having introduced monasticism, and also having brought in a new fashion of reciting the Psalms. Basil answered these charges, not because he desired the bishopric, but because he was unwilling to be falsely accused. He cleared himself of false teaching; he explained that he had not been the inventor of the monastic state, which had long been flourishing in Egypt and Palestine; and that, as to the way of reciting the Psalms by alternate verses, which he had established, this also had long been in use in many parts of the Church. Basil was not desirous to take a more prominent part than he was doing in the management of the Church, but he explained that if it were necessary for him to do so it would not be to Neocæsarea that he would feel his labours due, but to his own native city of Cæsarea, in Cappadocia.

And here, indeed, he was now most urgently needed. Eusebius, the bishop, was, as has been said, a man by no means skilled in questions of religious doctrine, and the Arians had taken advantage of this to spread their tenets, and as usual with them, to involve all things in confusion. A wise and prudent champion for the orthodox views was sorely needed, and all men saw that none was so fit as Basil.

Being made acquainted with the desire of the bishop and all his friends that he should return among them, Basil at once yielded, and leaving his beloved solitudes, came to take up his abode at Cæsarea. In the earnest labours which he now commenced, in his preaching and teaching, in his establishment of hospitals for the sick and suffering, and houses of religious retirement for those who desired them, Basil was heartily assisted by his friend Gregory, and the Bishop Eusebius was ready to be guided by him in all things that he suggested for the good of the Church. It came about that the exertions of Basil were speedily required, not only for the spiritual instruction of the Church at Cæsarea, but also for the supply of bodily necessaries.

A strange series of calamities fell just now upon this city and country. Storms of hailstones, of a size unknown before, destroyed the crops; inundations devastated the country, and earthquakes spread terror and ruin in the land. Then came a terrible famine; and the holders of corn keeping it up with a hard-hearted eagerness to obtain higher prices, the poor were quickly dying of starvation. Only the energy and devotion of Basil saved them from utter destruction. By his powerful appeals he obtained large gifts of money from the rich, which enabled him to procure provisions and to open large buildings, where he received all that were in pressing need and fed them, while at the same time he also busied himself in administering spiritual teaching to the poor and ignorant.

Another sort of trial was now to come upon Basil. The Emperor Valens, who was entirely devoted to the Arians, determined now to use all his influence for the furtherance of their views. An officer of his came to Cæsarea, and tried every means to make Basil favourable to their cause, promising him that he should be at once raised to the bishopric, in place of Eusebius. Basil, however, was not for a moment to be shaken, or induced in any way to favour the false doctrine of Arius. As to the place of bishop, he did not desire it, but was quite contented to labour for the good of the Church under the government of Eusebius. Soon, however, the post of highest dignity in the Church came to Basil in a legitimate manner—Eusebius died in the arms of Basil, and at once the eyes of all the orthodox party were turned towards Basil as his successor. The Arians, who were numerous and powerful, made a great opposition, but the orthodox prevailed in carrying the election, and about the year 370 A.D. Basil was consecrated to the important archiepiscopal see of Cæsarea. It was not the love of earthly honour or earthly riches that had induced him to take the office of a bishop, and he soon found that these were not to be expected in the post to which he had been promoted.

The Emperor was a strong partisan of the opinions to which Basil was earnestly opposed, and Modestus, the Governor of Cæsarea, to please him, threatened and attacked Basil in every way to make him submit to the teaching of the Arians. But Basil stood firm. " You threaten me," he said to the governor, " with confiscation of goods, torture, and death, but none of these things can hurt me. Confiscation is nothing to one who has nothing to lose, banishment I regard not who am tied to no place. I account not this country where I now dwell mine own; and I can think any country to be mine where I shall be cast. The whole earth is God's, whose pilgrim and wayfarer I am. Your tortures would be nothing for a body which would sink at once from its feebleness; and as to death, it will but send me the sooner to God, whose I am and whom I serve." With such an undaunted spirit did the bishop meet the threatenings of the governor, that this latter at once saw that he was not to be brought to yield, and reported to the Emperor accordingly. He told him at the same time that Basil had an equal contempt for rewards and offers of benefits as he had for threats, and Valens, who was not without some noble qualities, admired this man of so brave and constant a spirit.

Being at Cæsarea about the time of Christmas, the Emperor attended the public service in the church where Basil presided, and was so struck by the beauty and solemnity of the service, that he had much conversation with Basil upon the great doctrines of the faith, and seemed inclined to become altogether favourable to him. But the Arian bishops, who watched the Emperor closely, were determined to prevent this. They represented to Valens that Basil's virtues and wisdom made him especially dangerous to their cause, and a great obstacle to the spread of Arian doctrines, and they induced the Emperor to promise to banish him. It is said, however, that when Valens took in hand the pen to sign the sentence, it broke in his hand, and a second having done the same, the Emperor was so struck and terrified by the strange occurrence, that he would no more attempt to sign the warrant. However this may be, Basil escaped banishment, and the favour of the Emperor again returned to him. Before he left Cæsarea, he gave him several rich farms, which Basil received with joy, to be used for the sick and the poor.

The Emperor now left Cæsarea, and went to Antioch; but the governor of the province continued to molest Basil, while the people were so devotedly attached to him, that on one occasion the governor nearly lost his life in a popular tumult, which had been stirred up by the unjust treatment which Basil had received. As soon as Basil was a little relieved from the persecution of the civil officers of the empire, he set himself earnestly to reform the abuses which had grown up in his own Church. He was the head or presiding bishop of the diocese, but under him there were many country bishops, who, it seems, had been guilty of great negligence in admitting persons into the ministry without any proper qualifications, in order that they might escape the military service, and also of doing this for sums of money. Basil severely condemned these malpractices, especially the latter, which he pointed out was the sin for which Simon Magus was so bitterly reproved by St. Peter. Basil also, like Hilary, and others of the greater fathers, did not confine his views to the Church over which he himself was placed, but sought to do good anywhere in the Church of Christ where he saw an opportunity.

Very miserable disputes and dissensions were now vexing the Church at Antioch, and to the Christians there Basil sent an earnest letter of admonition. Valens being dead, an orthodox Emperor now reigned over the East, and Basil received a commission to visit the Churches in Armenia, to settle the confusion which had been introduced by heresy and persecution. In attempting to do this, he was involved in many disputes and quarrels, out of which grew an accusation, very generally believed, that Basil had deserted the orthodox faith, and in particular, had denied the Divinity of the Holy Ghost. The ground for this accusation was that Basil, in using the Doxology at the end of his sermons, had sometimes used it thus:—"Glory to the Father *with* the Son and the Holy Ghost;" or thus—"Glory to the Father, *by* the Son *in* the Holy Ghost." These expressions would not have attracted so much attention, were it not for the universal prevalence of errors on the doctrine of the Trinity at that time. That Basil did not use the words in any unorthodox sense he clearly explained to his friend Gregory, and afterwards he wrote a treatise on the subject of "The Holy Spirit," in which he more fully sets forth the orthodox doctrine.

But no man of note in those unquiet days could long escape accusations against his faith or morals from some who ought to have acted as his brethren. The Arian heresy seems to have poisoned the whole Christian atmosphere. Interminable slanders, libels, insinuations, attacks were going on among the bishops and clergy of the Church, and far more deadly to the cause of religion were the bad passions shown among churchmen themselves than the most fierce and cruel attacks of heathen persecution had proved in the century before. A letter of Basil to one of his calumniators complains bitterly of this iniquity of the age, which entertained every calumny and slander, and encouraged and fostered quarrels, divisions, and evil speakings. In the midst of all this malice and enmity, the beautiful friendship which continued to subsist unbroken between Basil and Gregory of Nazianzum is the more to be admired. Their mutual love and unbroken confidence must have been indeed cheering to both of them in the midst of the turmoils of the period in which they lived, and often doubtless did these two holy men sigh for the time when, released from all the distractions of this world, they might live together in love for ever.

The summons of release came to Basil first. He had governed the Church of Cæsarea but eight years when his weak and frail body, broken by austerities, and by the workings of the mighty spirit which it held, suddenly failed. Finding himself sinking, he mustered strength enough to ordain some in whom he had especial confidence, that they might carry on his work after him, and then he was forced to take to his bed. On the news of his illness, the people flocked from all quarters to catch a last glimpse of their beloved pastor, and to offer up prayers for him. Basil, fast sinking, addressed with difficulty a pious exhortation to those around him, and then, with the words, "Into Thy hands I commend my spirit," fell asleep. A.D. 379. He was little more than fifty years of age, but he was already an old man in strength and vigour of body, so constant had been his labours and self-denial. A very touching epitaph was written on his friend by Gregory of Nazianzum, in which he sets forth the loss which the whole Church had experienced by the death of such a man, and his own bitter sorrow at being parted from him for a season.

ST. GREGORY NAZIANZEN.

The life of Gregory of Nazianzum cannot be separated from that of Basil, in relating which we have already spoken of the close and intimate friendship which subsisted from boyhood to the grave between these two holy men. They were both natives of Cappadocia, Gregory having been born at Nazianzum, of which place his father was bishop, in the year 329. As the son of a Christian bishop and of a mother also of remarkable piety, Gregory may be supposed to have had the most full advantages in his early training, yet it is very remarkable that he was not baptized until of adult age; and, on the occasion of being in great peril of his life in a storm on his voyage to Athens, Gregory suffered the most acute terrors, from the consciousness of his not having been admitted by that sacrament into the privileges of Christianity. He became acquainted with Basil in early youth, having been sent to Cæsarea to study there, and their subsequent course of life was much the same; Gregory also having been sent to Cæsarea, in Palestine, and to Alexandria, in Egypt, to acquire rhetoric and philosophy, and then having repaired to Athens, to complete his education, he there, as has been already said, formed the closest intimacy with Basil. At Athens he gained so high a reputation, that he was prevailed upon to remain after Basil had quitted it, in order publicly to profess the art of rhetoric. In this employment he gained much credit, but he was not satisfied to remain long absent from his country and his parents; and at thirty years of age he left the famous University of Athens, and journeyed homewards through Constantinople. At Constantinople he found his brother Cæsarius, who though a physician of great reputation there, was willing to abandon his high prospects of fame and wealth, and to return home with Gregory to their parents in Cappadocia. Up to the time of his return Gregory had still remained unbaptized, though a zealous Christian in his way of living. He was now admitted into the Church by that sacrament, and soon afterwards ordained a presbyter of the Church by his father, then Bishop of Nazianzum.

The elder Gregory, who was not a very profound theologian, had been led by the Arian party into subscribing a form of faith which did not oppose their errors, and in consequence the orthodox had left his communion. Gregory the son was now able, by his learning and eloquence, to convince his father of his mistake, and to prevail upon him to undo it, and then to reconcile to him those who had taken up a position of hostility. On this occasion he pronounced one of those orations which have been preserved to us, and which are very striking compositions, uniting the eloquence of the practised orator with deep knowledge of Christian doctrine and piety.

Gregory had not been long living with his father before he was earnestly invited by Basil to join him in his solitary retreat in the mountains of Pontus, of which mention was made in the life of Basil. As his brother Cæsarius was living at home, to take care of his aged parents, Gregory was able to allow himself the pleasure of joining his friend in his quiet and studious life, which, under the circumstances of the time and the great needs of the Church, was certainly in both him and Basil, an act of self-indulgence though perhaps a justifiable one. Here he passed some years in sacred study and ascetic practices. His father, weighed down by increasing infirmities, had often entreated him to return and assist him, but from this, which seems to have been his manifest duty, Gregory had long shrunk.

The passion for a monastic life appears often to blind good men to simple duties, which are plain to other people. At length, however, he yielded, and in order to excuse himself from the charges which were naturally enough made against him, for having so long persevered in living in solitude, he published an "Apology," in which he eloquently dwells upon the charms of solitude and the great difficulties and responsibilities of the ministerial office. He does not appear to see that it is only the cowardly soldier who runs away from a post because it is difficult and dangerous, and that the very fact of its difficulty ought to make all such well-prepared combatants as he was ready to play their part manfully. However, now that he had returned to active life, Gregory gave himself up to a diligent performance of his ministerial duties, and as assistant to his aged father, laboured to convince gainsayers and to forward the great work of the Christian Church.

We now come to a part of the life of Gregory which is not so creditable to him, and which lets us see plainly the especial weakness of this great man, namely, a nervous sensibility and shrinking from encountering difficulties. His old and intimate friend, Basil, now Archbishop of Cæsarea, had formed a new see at an obscure place called Sasima, and for certain reasons he was very anxious that Gregory should be consecrated to be bishop of this place. The proposal, however, annoyed Gregory beyond measure. He wrote angrily to Basil, telling him that he desired quiet and retirement, and also objecting to the insignificance of the place which he proposed to him for a bishopric. He accuses Basil of being swelled with pride by his promotion; says that he is not aware that he is in anything superior to himself, and declares that he can never trust friendship any more. Basil, however, would not be offended by this very violent letter, nor would he abandon his attempt. He induced Gregory's father to join with him in entreaties that Gregory would allow himself to be made Bishop of Sasima; and now Gregory yielded, making, as was his wont, in order to excuse himself, an apologetic oration, in which he seemed to give excellent reasons for his strange conduct. However, it appears that after all he could not satisfy himself, for though he was consecrated Bishop of Sasima, he refused to go there, and indeed never visited the see to which he had been promoted. It was, he says, a paltry town, close and narrow, full of post-horses and public carriages, being situate on three great roads; the air, soil, and water were bad; the people were vagrants; the place noisy and dirty. These complaints come with somewhat of a bad grace from one who had written up the charms of the life of asceticism.

The truth is that Gregory was excessively mortified at having such a small and insignificant charge thrust upon him, and could not forgive Basil, who had above fifty sees in his province, for having picked out such a mean one for his friend. Indignant and vexed both with himself and his friend, Gregory now retired into solitude, and it was only by the most urgent entreaties of his father that he was brought back to Nazianzum, the old man now desiring to resign his episcopal charge into the hands of his son. Gregory at last consented to undertake this work, on condition that when his father died he should be considered free. As soon as he had begun his charge at his native town, he gave proof of his wisdom and the power of his eloquence. A dangerous tumult had been excited among the people by the harshness of the governor, but the bishop was able, by his earnest appeals, to persuade the people to submit to authority, as well as to induce the governor to adopt more gentle courses. Indeed, no one can read the " Orations " of Gregory which have come down to us, without being struck by the great power which is displayed in these compositions. Gregory was emphatically an orator, and must have always produced a great effect when he addressed the people.

Gregory was now tried by many losses in his family. His brother Cæsarius, the famous physician, who had been raised by the Emperor to the highest dignity, had died some little time before; and now, soon after his beginning his work as bishop of Nazianzum, his sister Gorgonia died. She was a married lady with a large family, and is represented to have been a beautiful example of true Christian piety, exemplary in performing her duties, very devout and attentive to religion, and of great modesty in her dress and demeanour.

The aged Bishop of Nazianzum was greatly blessed in his family, all of whom would appear to have been of high merit. He had for forty-five years laboured as bishop, and now, with his son, whom he could wholly trust, as coadjutor, he was able to spare himself much of the fatigue of his duties. But his great age and numerous infirmities weighed him down soon after his son had come to help him, and he died aged nearly a hundred years, with the highest character for holiness and devotion.

On the occasion of his funeral, his son Gregory spoke one of the most famous of his orations, which was rendered more pointed and striking by the presence of Basil at the funeral. For, as if desirous now to do away with the effect of the hard terms he had lately used towards Basil, and the bitterness with which he had addressed him, Gregory laboured to bestow a most glowing panegyric upon him, some of which seems indeed unfit to be spoken in a Christian church of a weak and fallible man, sitting to listen to it. We can much more patiently read Gregory's laboured panegyric of his deceased father, nor are we revolted by the enthusiastic terms in which he speaks of his aged mother, who survived her husband, for here filial piety seems to excuse a great deal. The language indeed may appear to us somewhat exaggerated, as when he says, " I think that if any one had laboured to make the most excellent match out of the whole world and the entire race of men, that no more excellent and harmonious one could be possible than this. For all the most admirable properties, both of man and woman, became united together, in such a way that this was rather the marriage of absolute virtue than of human beings."

It is usual in the panegyrics made upon Christians in early times to find only the ascetic virtues and the devotion to religious services magnified; but Gregory says of his mother, " She was as clever and skilful in the temporal affairs of her house as if she knew nothing of piety ; and she was as much devoted to God and religion as though no domestic charge belonged to her."

The death of this good old lady took place not long after that of her husband, and Gregory, now that both of his parents were gone, thought himself entirely absolved from his promise to attend to the church at Nazianzum. There would have been no difficulty in his being regularly appointed to the see by Basil, the archbishop of the province, and without doubt Basil would have gladly appointed him to it; but Gregory seemed to shrink from the hard work and responsibility of the episcopal function in a small provincial town.

Perhaps, indeed, he longed for wider fame and a more distinguished field, and feeling conscious, as he did, of the great gifts of oratory which he possessed, was unwilling that his light should longer be hidden in Cappadocia. The death of his friend Basil was the severing of another tie which bound him to that part of the world, and though the see of Nazianzum was still without a bishop, yet it could not be said that he was actually bound to give his services to that church, inasmuch as he had expressly stipulated, when he became coadjutor to his father, that he should be free on his death. Accordingly Gregory now repaired to Constantinople, the splendid capital city of the empire, and prepared to employ his great talents for the upholding of the Christian faith there.

Great, indeed, was the need of preachers and divines such as Gregory at that moment in the capital city. The heresy of Arius, of which we have often had occasion to speak, had, under the encouragement of the Emperor Valens, almost overpowered the orthodox faith, and it was in order to provide a powerful champion on the side of the truth that a Council held at Antioch a short time before, where Gregory was present, had requested him to go to the capital city. On his coming there (about the year 379), he at once proceeded to preach in a private house belonging to a kinsman of his. His preaching attracted much attention, and produced marked effect; the house was soon changed into a church, called the Church of the Resurrection, which was densely thronged with hearers, and the heretical party, which then had all the power, immediately began to excite tumults against this dangerous opponent, and to make accusations against him before the magistrates. He was accused of teaching that there were Three Gods; he was assailed in the streets with stones and missiles, and his life was placed in danger. But Gregory did not shrink from what he knew was his plain duty. He felt that if men were against him, God was on his side, and that though they might have the stronger party, yet he had the better cause. The magistrates before whom he was brought could find no ground for punishing him, as the Emperor's edict allowed the orthodox to teach, and the effect of his persecution was to make him more widely known and to bring more to hear him.

It was now that one of the most famous of the Fathers of the Church, St. Jerome, was under his instruction, and greatly did he value, as he often tells us in his writings, the teaching of Gregory. The orthodox bishops throughout the East now desired that Gregory should be formally appointed bishop of those who held to the true faith in Constantinople, and this was done. Soon afterwards an Egyptian, named Maximus, a subtle and plausible person, who had imposed upon Gregory, and been well treated by him, took occasion of his temporary absence from the city to usurp the bishop's place, to which he was consecrated by some Egyptian bishops who were joined with him in the plot. A great tumult was raised by the friends of Gregory, and he himself returning, delivered one of his famous orations, in which he exposed the treachery of Maximus and defended his own life and doctrine. Maximus was obliged to fly, but he would not abandon his claim to the see, but perseveringly assailed both the synods of the Church and the Emperor, in order to obtain the post which he so much coveted, but without success.

Gregory, though delivered from this opponent, did not find all things go smoothly at Constantinople. He was not only reviled and attacked by the Arians, but some of his own people were drawn away from him, on the ground that he did not sufficiently try to protect them from the unjust usage of the civil power. Gregory, who was of a very timid and sensitive temper, and not well suited to contend with difficulties and contradictions, wished to withdraw at once from his sphere of duty; but the people would not hear of this, and by their earnest entreaties at length prevailed upon him to remain.

Theodosius had now succeeded to the throne of the Roman Empire, which he shared with Gratian and Valentinian. He was a prince devotedly attached to the orthodox religion, and though he had long delayed to receive baptism, yet being at Thessalonica, in Greece, and falling ill, he determined no longer to delay, but was baptized by the orthodox bishop of that place. After this he came to Constantinople, determined to overthrow the Arians, and having published a decree commanding all men to follow the true Catholic faith, he gave warning to the Arian clergy to give up their churches, and when they had abandoned them, he installed Gregory, with great honour and dignity, as bishop of the Church, and treated him with the most marked deference.

The bishop's presence was eagerly desired at Court, but Gregory, who always loved retirement, shrank from these public scenes and sought for solitude. The temporal affairs of his see he would not intermeddle with, but left all the care of them to others. He thus showed his disregard for grandeur and riches; but we cannot agree with his biographers, that he is to be commended for shrinking from what was his clear and manifest duty, such as a due attendance at the Court of the Emperor, and a careful administration of the revenues of his see. Much more ready are we to acknowledge his Christian charity in so readily and kindly forgiving one who acknowledged that he had been hired to assassinate him.

The Emperor, in pursuance of his design to restore the orthodox faith, and to overthrow heresy, now proceeded to summon a General Council of all the bishops of the East, to meet at Constantinople. 150 orthodox bishops obeyed his summons, as well as 36 who held the Macedonian heresy, which taught erroneous doctrine concerning the Holy Ghost. This important Council met in May 381, and its decrees have always been and are still accepted as binding on the whole Church. Its first work was to settle the disputes concerning the see of Constantinople. It decided that Maximus had no claim to the see; that Gregory of Nazianzum was the true bishop, the Arian bishop having been deposed, and they confirmed Gregory in all the rights of this high and dignified post. It was objected at the time that Gregory was translated from Nazianzum, and that one of the canons of the Council of Nice had forbidden translations; but Gregory replied that he had never been actual bishop of Nazianzum, but only coadjutor and assistant, and as to his other see of Sasima, he had never occupied it. The Council then proceeded to discuss matters of faith, and first it ratified the Nicene Creed, which so expressly condemns the heresy of Arius. But as the Macedonian heresy on the nature of the Third Person in the Trinity needed also to be now condemned, the Constantinopolitan Council added a considerable portion to the Nicene Creed. The first Creed had stopped with the words "and the Holy Ghost;" that which followed after these words being an anathema against those who held doctrine opposed to what had been laid down in the Creed. The Constantinople Creed, in place of this anathema, added all the words after "the Holy Ghost" which we now recite in our Church service—all the words, with one important exception. In the Constantinople Creed the words "and the Son" do not occur; nor were these words put into any Creed of the Church until about the year 613; nor were they then inserted on any authority, but, as far as it appears, by accident. The Creed was generally used without them until the beginning of the ninth century, when a dispute having arisen as to the question of the procession of the Holy Ghost, and a Council having met at Aix (809), certain bishops were sent to the Pope to request that these words—"and the Son"—might be inserted in the Creed. The Pope, however, refused, and caused the Creed, without this addition, to be engraved on silver tablets and hung up behind the altar of St. Peter. At a synod held at Arles (813) a Creed was published with the words added. Finally, in the time of Pope Nicholas I. (858), they appear to have got permanent possession in the Creed, and to have caused the indignant protests of the Greeks, with whom, as is well known, this addition to the Creed was one principal cause of their separation from the Latin Church.

We have digressed on this point, as it is one of much importance, and very interesting to us at the present day. Having agreed to their important confession of faith, which indirectly condemned all the heresies then prevalent, the Fathers of the Council thought it expedient to add special condemnations or anathemas against these heresies separately. They then applied themselves to the important subject of the arrangement of the sees of bishops in certain great divisions, which came to be called patriarchates, but were originally called dioceses, from the name used in the civil government. These divisions were five, according to the divisions of the secular government, and the bishops of each division were to transact the affairs of the Church in the division in which they were placed, under the presidency of one chief bishop, called the metropolitan or patriarch. The bishops of Constantinople, Antioch and Alexandria were always to have this rank. The see of Constantinople was to rank first, next after that of Rome, because, as the Council said, Constantinople is "new Rome." This arrangement is important, inasmuch as it shows clearly the cause of the early precedence which was given to the see of Rome, and on which such a vast edifice of false claims was afterwards built up. Rome had a certain precedence, because the city of Rome was the ancient capital of the empire, and not on the ground of the see having a higher authority than other sees, much less on its having authority to intrude into other patriarchates. The General Council of Chalcedon, in the next century, decreed that the bishops of Rome and Constantinople were to be held equal, inasmuch as both of them were bishops of capital cities. The Council of Constantinople, which had for some time proceeded harmoniously, now began to fall into quarrels and disputes, and a great faction was formed against Gregory Nazianzen, declaring that he had not been canonically promoted to the see of Constantinople. Gregory acted according to his usual manner. Sensitive and shrinking to an excess, at the first word of opposition he sought to resign his trust, and having, though with difficulty, obtained from the Emperor permission to do so, he pronounced a splendid and most touching oration before the Council and the people, who were in the utmost sorrow at losing him.

In this part of pathetic oratory Gregory is great, perhaps unrivalled. He appealed to them, like Samuel, to witness of his integrity. He declared that he had not sought theirs but them. "Believe your guide," he exclaimed, "whom you were never wont to disbelieve; I am weary while my mildness and moderation are charged upon me as a fault; I am weary while I am forced to encounter with rumours and envy; and not only with enemies, but with friends, who wound more deeply and securely. I beseech you, by all that is dear and sacred, do me this kindness, to dismiss me with your prayers; let that be the reward of my conflicts and trials; grant me a warrant for my discharge, as generals are wont to do for their worn-out soldiers. And as for a successor, God will provide Himself a pastor, as once He did a lamb for a burnt-offering. I only beg of you that you would choose such an one as may be the object rather of men's envy than their pity, who may not be ready basely to comply with every one upon all occasions, but willing to venture the favour and the frowns of men in doing what is just and true." He then addresses his Church of the Resurrection, in which the orthodox revival had first begun, the "great and venerable temple," the cathedral of the city, and all the other churches "which approached it in splendour and beauty," and bids them farewell. He says farewell to the assembly of bishops, to the clergy, the widows, the virgins, to the poor, to the sick, to those who had so eagerly hung upon his words as a preacher, to all who had loved and cared for him. Not often has a more touching farewell sermon been preached than Gregory then delivered, and greatly was his audience affected by it; nor indeed would they have suffered him to retire, had he not begged and entreated them to do so, and showed them both that it was his own desire and also highly advantageous to the peace of the Church. So, after three years' important and eventful work in the great city of Constantinople, Gregory again returned in peace to his native Cappadocia.

It was but natural that Gregory should have left Constantinople with no very good opinion of the value of Councils, for certainly the Council of Constantinople had not used him well; and so, when the next year he was invited to attend another synod at that city, he refused somewhat peevishly, declaring that he had never known any good come from assemblies of bishops, although, in the latter part of his letter (Ep. 55), he adds that he was suffering from severe illness, which would not have allowed him to go even if he had been so minded. Gregory was, as we have seen, of a very sensitive as well as timid disposition, and no doubt the slights which had been put upon him at Constantinople sank deep into his mind. It is however to use somewhat too strong language to compare, as he does in one of his poems, the grave synods of bishops to flocks of cackling geese. He had left, as we have seen, the see of Nazianzum vacant when he went to Constantinople, being not actually bound to take charge of it, although there were some good reasons why he should have done so. On his return, he found it still vacant, and in consequence the Church there full of all manner of error and heresy. The state of his health now furnished him with a valid excuse for declining the charge, but on his representation the Archbishop of Cæsarea consecrated a bishop for the long vacant see.

Having seen the wants of the Church thus provided for, Gregory could with greater ease and comfort devote himself to the solitude which he so much loved. The remainder of his days was past in sacred studies, and in poetical compositions on divine subjects. The history of his own life he wrote in Iambic verse. Before his death he had made a will leaving all his property, which was considerable, for the benefit of the poor at Nazianzum. This was in accordance with the spirit of his life, for he had always shown a most kind and charitable disposition. He had striven to promote Christian love and unity, and though not endowed with those qualities which produce great effects in the world, yet in his meekness, gentleness, and humility he had set a bright example. As a preacher and speaker he was eloquent, fervid, impetuous. The writings of Gregory, compared in their style with those of his contemporary and dear friend, Basil, seem somewhat inflated and bombastic; but this, which we consider a defect, was in his days held a high merit, and Gregory was considered in his time, as he has usually been since, one of the greatest writers and orators of the Christian Church.

ST. AMBROSE.

AMBROSE, a man famous in the history of the Church for wisdom, eloquence, and courage, was born about A.D. 333, at Arles, in France, where his father was military governor. Various stories are told of his childhood, as though presages were given as to his future greatness; but what we know for certain is, that he was well and carefully educated, and that at Rome, where his family went to reside, he speedily obtained distinction as a pleader, and gained the favour of Anicius Probus, the Prefect of Italy. By this high officer he was appointed governor of the district which lies around Milan, and in that famous and beautiful city he went to live. Milan at this period was one of the usual residences of the Emperor of the West; it was renowned for its buildings, its prosperity, and its learning, and the post of governor in so distinguished a city was one of high honour and dignity. This eminent place Ambrose filled to the complete satisfaction of all.

The Church at Milan had suffered from the all-pervading Arian heresy as other Churches had. Indeed Auxentius, the bishop, had been one of the special leaders of those evil opinions, and on this ground had been several times synodically deposed from his high place by the bishops who remained orthodox. But he obstinately refused to yield, and being supported by the Arian faction, maintained his hold on the archiepiscopal see until his death, which took place in the year 374. The Emperor Valentinian directed the bishops of the province to choose a successor, and bade them select a man who should not only be remarkable for his wisdom and learning, but also for virtuous and holy character, so that he might guide as much by example as by precept. Great difficulties, however, stood in the way of their selecting any one from among their own body to the high dignity of Archbishop of Milan. There was a large party among them who favoured more or less the Arian views, and these were bitterly hostile to all who had taken a strong line against these heresies in time past. Probably also there was no man of commanding distinction among these, and thus the assembled bishops were sorely perplexed how to proceed with the election. Meantime the people of the city, who took a lively interest in the choice, and were divided between the Arian and the orthodox sentiments, began to show symptoms of disorder and tumult. They thronged the church where the election was being made in a threatening manner, and Ambrose, as the civil governor of the city, was called upon to go to the place to preserve order. He delivered a grave oration to the people, exhorting them to preserve peace and concord. At that moment, it is said that the voice of a child was heard from the midst of the crowd exclaiming, " Ambrose is bishop!" The words seemed to the perplexed bishops like a message from heaven. Both the Arians and the orthodox saw in the suggestion a way out of all their difficulties. Ambrose, as a layman, was not specially committed to any religious party, and by his election neither side could be said to gain a triumph over the other. So all the bishops with one voice exclaimed that Ambrose should be bishop.

No one, perhaps, was so much astonished at this as Ambrose himself. It is certain that the thought of being a bishop had never entered his mind until that moment. He was a layman, employed in a civil office, and not only so, he was actually unbaptized at that time, although he had been carefully educated in Christian doctrine, and was then in the position of a catechumen, or one under instruction. We have had occasion to observe several times how prevalent the great fault of the delay of baptism was at that time. Ambrose was forty-one years of age when he was chosen bishop. He had been brought up in a Christian family, and yet, like Gregory of Nazianzum and the Emperor Theodosius, like Nectarius, chosen soon after this Bishop of Constantinople, Eusebius of Cæsarea, and many others in this age, he was unbaptized. The reason for delaying baptism in this way was that, as it was held that all sins were remitted in baptism, it was thought more secure to keep it in reserve until a person had actually determined on devoting himself to a religious life, than to seek it when there was fear lest, after receiving it, some fall into gross sin might take place. This seems to be taking an entirely false view of the grace of God, as several of the Christian Fathers did not fail to point out. There were also other reasons why Ambrose should not be chosen bishop besides the strangeness of the matter. The Council of Nice had expressly forbidden this very thing, and ordained that before any one should be admitted into holy orders, he should pass some time as a catechumen, and a longer time of probation after baptism. Of course the bishops assembled knew this, and in quiet times and under ordinary circumstances they would not perhaps have made the choice they did. The circumstances, however, and the great virtue of the man, seemed to excuse the irregularity.

But Ambrose himself shrank from yielding to what he rightly held was a most extraordinary proceeding. He took all the measures possible to defeat the intention of the bishops, and if it be true, as is said, that some of these measures were to try to make himself appear cruel and wicked, it seems difficult to justify him altogether. Finding, however, that these deceptive proceedings were seen through, he fled away and concealed himself; and it was only when the Emperor, who highly approved the choice, issued strict and threatening edicts against any who connived at his retreat, that he was discovered and brought back to Milan. He then submitted to what he judged was a special dispensation of Providence, was baptized, and eight days after solemnly consecrated to the see of Milan. The Emperor, who was present, was deeply interested in the ceremony, and publicly thanked God, that one whom he had chosen to set over the people in temporal things, should now be selected to govern them in spiritual things. Everywhere throughout the Church the news of the consecration of Ambrose was received with pleasure and satisfaction. St. Basil wrote him a letter full of high commendations, exhorting him to go boldly forward, to extirpate the Arian errors and revive the better times of the Gospel.

Ambrose at once gave himself up entirely to the duties of his office. He disposed his temporal goods in such a way that the care of them would not distract him, and sending for Simplicius, a Roman presbyter, of whose learning and virtue he thought very highly, he applied himself diligently to the study of theology under his direction. Very soon he was able himself to become an instructor. Little more than two years after his consecration, he put forth a book on the duties of those who had devoted themselves to a virgin life, a commentary on St. Luke, and a moral treatise called "Offices," in imitation of Cicero. Soon after this an invasion of the barbarian Goths, who broke into Italy, devastating all before them, forced Ambrose to retire from Milan, and to take refuge in Illyricum. As soon as the defeat of the Goths by the Emperor's general had removed the danger, he returned.

But new dangers and troubles of a more trying kind awaited him. Justina, widow of the Emperor Valentinian, and mother of the young Emperor who bore the same name, was a strong favourer of the Arian views, although during the lifetime of her husband she had concealed her opinions. She now incited the young Emperor to demand that some of the churches should be given up to the Arians; but this Ambrose firmly and successfully withstood. She further attempted to give support to Arianism by appointing a bishop of those opinions to the see of Sirmium, which had fallen vacant. Ambrose immediately repaired to the place, and either by his boldness and energy, or, as is said, in consequence of a striking calamity which befel one of the supporters of the Arian party, made such an impression on the people, that they rejected the Arian who had been appointed by the Empress, and allowed Ambrose to consecrate an orthodox bishop to the vacant see. He thus showed himself a man not to be daunted or stopped when he saw the path of duty clear before him; and the Christian courage which was so remarkable a characteristic of this holy bishop, though it might anger and vex those who were in authority, yet, nevertheless, made them, in spite of themselves, entertain the highest respect for the man who took so consistent a course. He, on the contrary, although he feared not the face of man when he saw that his duty required him to act, and was ready to withstand the highest power when it was illegally employed and used against God, was nevertheless most ready to serve the State to the utmost of his power, and at the cost of any difficulty and danger.

At this time Maximus, one of the generals of the empire, raised a rebellion against Gratian and the young Valentinian, and the former, advancing at the head of his army to meet him, was enticed into an ambush and barbarously murdered. Then Maximus with his soldiers ravaged all the country on the other side of the Alps, and prepared to march into Italy. Upon this the Empress, thoroughly frightened, applied herself in her need to the courageous Archbishop of Milan, and begged him to undertake an embassy to the conqueror, to endeavour to stop him on his way. Ambrose did not hesitate a moment, but at once undertook the office, and by his earnest appeals and arguments succeeded in preventing Maximus from advancing against Italy.

The confusion which the rising of Maximus caused in the empire, encouraged the favourers of the old heathen religion, which was not yet extinct, to extort from the young Emperor Valentinian II. a permission for their superstitious rites to be again publicly celebrated in the country. A learned and eloquent Roman, called Symmachus, who was governor of the city, was the chief mover in the matter. But as soon as Ambrose heard of the attempt, he wrote most strongly to the Emperor against it. He told him that to give any public encouragement to heathenism, would be to deny the sovereignty of God, and an act of apostasy for one who professed the Christian faith. He reminded him of the dreadful persecutions which the heathens had carried on against the Christians, and of the many edicts of the Christian Emperors, by which they had done away with all legal sanction to their belief. He told him that if he allowed the altar of victory to be raised in the senate, as the heathen prayed him to do, he could not be regarded as a Christian. No Christian bishop could minister to him the Sacraments, and he would bring disgrace on the memory of his father, who was a good Christian, and on that of his brother Gratian, lately murdered, who had done so much for the establishment of the Christian religion in the land. The young Emperor at once yielded to this remonstrance, if indeed he had ever intended to grant the petition of the heathen governor; and in order to confirm him against such representations, and to show how weak the cause of the heathen was, Ambrose wrote a reply at length to the document sent by Symmachus, in which, with admirable eloquence and force, he exposes the vanity of the heathen worship, and shows the solid foundation on which Christianity rests.

Symmachus was thus foiled by Ambrose, in his attempt to revive the dying ashes of Paganism, and we cannot but rejoice that it was so. But we owe to Symmachus nevertheless a debt of gratitude, for it was he that, struck by the talents of a young African orator, who was then giving lectures at Rome, engaged him to go to

Milan, where a professor of rhetoric was needed. This young African was no other than the great Augustine, the most famous of all the Christian Fathers, and his being sent to Milan was, under God, the cause of his being converted to the right faith from the false Manichean sentiments which he then held, and made to devote himself henceforth to the service of the Church, in which he fought a good warfare.

Augustine, on his arriving at Milan, went of course to hear the famous bishop preach, and the burning eloquence and zeal of Ambrose at once impressed his earnest nature. He was soon led to discard the vain and blasphemous notions which he held, to become truly penitent for his past life, which had been very irregular, and to receive baptism from the hands of Ambrose; after which he returned a thoroughly changed man to his native Africa.

But now severer trials were coming upon the good bishop who had been instrumental in doing so much for the Church. The Empress had never let go the notion of obtaining for the Arians, whom she favoured, equal rights of worship with the orthodox. Accordingly, she now induced the Emperor to make a law (A.D. 386) that the Arians might hold their public services without interruption, and that whoever attempted to hinder them should be held guilty of high treason. Great endeavours were made by the Court party to carry this law into effect, but Ambrose firmly opposed it, and his people so eagerly and heartily supported him, that it could not then be enforced. Equally firm was the good bishop against an attempt to entrap him into a public disputation with an Arian bishop, before judges already prejudiced on the side opposed to him. Nothing now remained for the Empress and the Arian party but to endeavour to seize by force the church which they coveted. An officer was sent, while Ambrose was performing the service, to demand its surrender. It so happened that one of the lessons for the day was that which gives the account of Ahab seizing upon Naboth's vineyard. Taking occasion from this, Ambrose boldly declared that as Naboth had refused to surrender the inheritance of his fathers, so would he not surrender the inheritance of his Lord. The people, though terrified by the threats of those in power, yet remained faithful to their bishop; and it is said that their courage was specially supported and sustained by the chanting of the Psalms in alternate verses, ending each with the doxology, a custom then newly introduced into that church by Ambrose from the East, where it had long prevailed.*

Many arrests were now made of those who would not yield to the Emperor's mandate, and the city was full of confusion. An Arian presbyter was seized by the people, and would have been torn in pieces, had not Ambrose come to his aid; the soldiers sent to seize and guard the churches showed themselves distinctly on the side of Ambrose and the Catholics, and so utterly impossible was it to quench the enthusiasm which was excited for the holy bishop, that the Court party was at length obliged to yield, and suffer the orthodox to retain their churches. Bitterly indeed did they feel towards the undaunted champion of the truth, who had thus successfully withstood the entrance of error among his people; but in a very short time the man who was so reviled and attacked became needed by the Empress and her son, and with a true Christian charity he showed himself ready to undertake the employment which they desired him to perform for them, though the danger

* See Life of St. Basil.

which he incurred in doing so was considerable. The usurper Maximus again threatened to invade Italy, and Ambrose was dispatched to try to arrest his progress as he had done before. At Trèves, on the banks of the Moselle, he was admitted to an audience with Maximus. Ambrose was a man whom nothing could daunt or affright. He boldly reproached Maximus with the crimes of which he had been guilty, and of his making war upon a youthful Emperor and his widowed mother. His embassy, however, proved unsuccessful, and he returned to Milan.

Meantime Maximus advanced, and seizing on the passes of the Alps, transported his army into Italy. The young Valentinian and his mother, struck with terror, fled away to Theodosius, the Emperor of the East, to implore his aid. After some delay, Theodosius espoused their cause heartily, and marching an army into Northern Italy, surprised and captured Maximus at Aquileia, and causing him to be beheaded, restored Valentinian and his mother to their former state. Nothing was more remarkable in St. Ambrose than the bold and intrepid manner in which he rebuked temporal rulers, when he judged them to have offended against the divine laws; and such was the holiness of his own life, and the sacredness of his character, that these exhortations were generally taken in good part, and produced wholesome effects in those to whom they were addressed. That Ambrose was sometimes, in his zeal for the Church, led to overlook the requirements of justice is not to be denied. This seems certainly to have been the case when he interfered in the matter of some Christians who had burned down a Jewish synagogue in a riot, and were ordered by the Emperor to rebuild it out of their own funds. Ambrose was so shocked at the notion of a place of false worship being built out of Christian funds, that he could not see the plain justice of the Christians being called upon to replace what they had unjustly destroyed, and the Emperor Theodosius yielded to his urgent entreaties.

But he was now to show himself as a bold champion for the right in a matter where all must confess that he deserves the highest praise. A riot had taken place at Thessalonica, and some of the Emperor's officers had been slain, and others ill-treated. Upon news of this being brought to Theodosius, the Eastern Emperor, who was still staying at Milan, he was exceedingly enraged, and ordered a general massacre of the people of the city. Ambrose hearing of this, earnestly opposed the unjust sentence, and on his powerful appeal to him, the Emperor promised that it should not be carried out. But when Ambrose was gone, the courtiers of Theodosius persuaded him to return to his former violence, and the order was sent to the soldiers at Thessalonica to put the inhabitants of the town to the sword. A dreadful massacre followed—the innocent and guilty perished together, and nearly 7,000 persons were put to death. The good Bishop of Milan was horrified at this great crime committed by the order of a Christian Emperor, and he determined to show to the prince, that though his power was great and his station high, yet that the laws of God were greater than he, and that he could not be permitted to outrage them with impunity. He immediately addressed a letter to Theodosius, pointing out to him the heinousness of the sin which he had committed, and exhorting him to a public and sincere repentance, at the same time telling him that he could not admit him to the sacraments of the Church before his repentance was fully shown. Theodosius, who was a prince of a noble disposition, though easily led away by passion, was struck by the letter, and came to the church at Milan where Ambrose was officiating, intending probably to hold a conference on the matter of the letter with Ambrose. But at the church door he was met by the intrepid bishop, who forbade him to enter the house of God stained as he was by the guilt of unrepented murder. "Perhaps, sire," he said, "you do not rightly apprehend the horrible nature of the massacre lately committed, for though the storm of your fury be blown over, yet reason has not yet recovered its sight to discern clearly the greatness of the mischief. The imperial lustre, perhaps, blinds your eyes that you cannot see your offence, and your power imposes upon your reason. But you would do well to look to the frail and corruptible condition of human nature, and to reflect upon that original dust out of which we were all made, and unto which we must all return. Let not the splendour of your purple robes hinder you from being acquainted with the infirmities of that body which they cover. You are, sire, of the same make with those subjects whom you govern, who are not your subjects only, but in some sense your fellow-servants. For there is one Lord and Emperor of the world, the great Creator of all things. And with what eyes then will you behold the temple of this common Lord? With what feet will you tread His sanctuary? How will you stretch forth those hands in prayer which are still reeking with the blood of the innocent? How will you presume with such hands to receive the most sacred body of our Lord? How will you lift up His most sacred blood to those lips which lately uttered so savage a decree for the unjust shedding of so much blood? Depart therefore, and seek not by a second offence to aggravate your former fault, but quietly take the yoke upon you which our great Lord has from above allotted for you. It is sharp, but it is healing, and well calculated to produce good effects." On receiving this plain and public rebuke from the minister of Christ, the Emperor stood for a moment amazed. Then he said that even David had been guilty both of murder and adultery. Ambrose replied, " Him whom you have followed in his sin, follow also in his repentance."

What could have been more striking than this

ST. AMBROSE RESISTING THEODOSIUS.—*Page* 196.

scene, or what more edifying to the vast number of persons who witnessed it. The majesty of God's eternal law was here righteously vindicated without fear of man, and He " who is no respecter of persons " had indeed ascribed to Him the " honour due unto His name."

Upon the Emperor the boldness of the bishop had an immediate and most salutary effect. Touched in his conscience for his sin, and acknowledging the justice of the treatment which he received from the minister of Christ, he retired to his palace, and testified his grief and penitence by tears and lamentations. Eight months did he remain as a penitent clad in the garments of mourning, and humbling himself on account of his sin. When Christmas came he lamented most bitterly that at that high season of Christian joy the gates of God's house were still closed against him. One of his courtiers persuaded him to go to the bishop and declare his penitence. This he did, but was at first rather roughly received by Ambrose, who would not grant him absolution until he had promised to make a salutary decree that no order of the Emperor touching life should be executed until after thirty days had elapsed, thus allowing time for passion to pass away, and for calm reason to consider the justice of the sentence. Ambrose then absolved the Emperor from the censures of the Church, and allowed him to come to the Holy Table.

Throughout these transactions the conduct of the bishop had been worthy of admiration, but when afterwards Theodosius presented himself in church, and according to the custom of the Emperors at Constantinople passed within the communion rails to receive the holy sacrament, Ambrose seems to have displayed towards him somewhat of arrogance and disrespect. He sent one of his deacons to order him to quit the place within the rails and to stand outside, for that though the purple made men emperors, it did not make them priests. Theodosius meekly complied, and explained to the bishop that he had not taken this place through arrogance, but because it was the custom to do so at Constantinople. Perhaps, under the circumstances, Ambrose might have shown a little more tenderness for the royal penitent.

Theodosius now quitted Milan and returned to the East, and the young Emperor Valentinian went into France on an expedition against some of the people of that country who were in arms against his authority. Count Arbogastes, the general of the forces in France, who was very popular with the soldiers, was found by the Emperor so overbearing and insubordinate, that he dismissed him from his command. The Count vowed vengeance, and soon afterwards Valentinian was found strangled in his palace. This dreadful crime was made more shocking by the special circumstances of the case. Valentinian, who had in his early youth favoured the Arians at his mother's bidding, had never been admitted by baptism into the Church, but had become most earnestly desirous to receive that sacrament. From Vienne, in France, where he was staying, he had sent to Milan earnestly pressing Ambrose to come to him to baptize him, and the good bishop had already set out on his journey and crossed the Alps, when he heard the sad news of the Emperor's murder. Greatly afflicted, he returned to Milan, and when the body of the young Emperor was brought there for burial, he preached a pathetic sermon, lamenting his untimely end, and declaring his belief that Valentinian would not suffer in the next world for the want of baptism, inasmuch as he had earnestly desired and sought it. He speaks of his brother Gratian, who had also been the victim of an assassin, welcoming the good young prince into the regions of the blessed, applying to them the words of Scripture—" They were lovely and pleasant in their lives, and in their death they were not divided."

Soon after this the Emperor Theodosius and Ambrose were again brought together by the expedition which the former made into Italy against Eugenius, who had seized on the empire of the West, and being a heathen, had threatened the Christians with destruction. Theodosius was completely successful against him, and he ascribed his success principally to the prayers of Ambrose. And now this good Emperor, who had ever been a true supporter of the Church, fell sick and saw his end approaching. His last illness was distinguished by various acts of clemency and charity, while the good bishop, who had once been so sternly opposed to him, now ministered to him with tender care. On his death (395 A.D.) Ambrose pronounced a long funeral oration, giving a just panegyric on his virtues. His sons Arcadius and Honorius succeeded him. To the latter the Western empire was assigned, and somewhat of ill feeling arose between him and Ambrose on account of a malefactor, condemned to be thrown to the wild beasts, who had taken refuge in a church, and was forcibly dragged from thence by the Emperor's soldiers. It was characteristic of Ambrose to place so highly the sanctity of the buildings dedicated to Christian worship, as to think that no amount of crime could justify a forcible capture in one of them. The right of sanctuary, which he so eagerly defended, has been a claim grossly abused and productive of many mischiefs; but it owes its origin to a highly commendable feeling, which ascribes to everything connected with the Most High an awful holiness, and forbids human power to trespass where Divine power especially sits enthroned.

The archbishop did not long survive the good Emperor Theodosius. In the beginning of the year 398 he began to sink, but he prophesied that he should live over Easter, and this proved to be true. In his sick bed he still occupied himself with his sacred studies, the last subject on which he was employed being a commentary on the 42nd Psalm, which he left unfinished. In his last hours he was attended by Honoratus,

Bishop of Vercellæ, from whom he received the holy communion, almost immediately before he expired. He had mentioned the name of the man whom he desired to succeed him, and this was singularly enough the presbyter Simplician, who had been his instructor in theology when he was made bishop, and who was an older man than Ambrose himself. The highest honours were paid to Ambrose at his burial, and he has ever since been regarded as one of the greatest men whom the early Church produced. His Christian courage and unflinching devotion to high principles have probably never been surpassed: if he was somewhat too rigid and overbearing, it was in a righteous cause, and out of zeal for his Master's service, not for any private or ambitious ends of his own. "He had indeed," says Dr. Cave, "a natural greatness and gallantry of mind that made him speak freely and boldly upon all occasions, nor was he by any considerations of fear or favour to be moved one hair's breadth where the cause of God and religion lay at stake; and yet none more indulgent to those who were truly penitent. When any came to him to confess their offences, he wept for them and with them, and by his own set their tears afloat." In the services of public worship he took especial delight, attending to their musical performance with the utmost care. He introduced, as has been mentioned, the chanting of the Psalms in alternate verses, and it is to him we owe that noble Christian hymn, the highest of uninspired songs of praise, which since his days has ever resounded, and will ever continue to resound, in the Christian Church—the *Te Deum laudamus.*

ST. JEROME.

HIERONYMUS, or Jerome, was confessedly the most learned, and in many ways the most remarkable of all the Fathers of the Christian Church. Inferior to St. Ambrose in weight of character, and to St. Augustine in the power of setting forth the inner Christian life; inferior to St. Chrysostom in genuine religious eloquence, he yet was a more powerful writer than either of them, and by his great knowledge of languages and his wonderful industry did more than any other man towards the interpretation of the Holy Scriptures He was a man not without serious faults, the chief of which were the extreme violence and bitterness of his temper towards those who differed from him, and sometimes a want of truthfulness and honesty in his controversies; but his zeal for religion, his devotion to good works, and his self-denying labours for the Church have perhaps never been surpassed.

Jerome was born at Stridon, a small town or

village in Dalmatia, about the year 346 A.D. His family professed the Christian religion, and was a well-ordered and virtuous household; it was also sufficiently wealthy. Jerome was instructed in his early youth by his father, and was then sent to Rome to complete his education, especially in the subjects, then most highly prized, of grammar and rhetoric. His first sight of that grand and famous city must doubtless have impressed the young Dalmatian as it has so many others. There were the mighty memorials of the ancient glory of Rome—palaces, amphitheatres, courts, aqueducts, statues, monuments. The spoils of the world adorned the capitol, and the triumphal arches reared in honour of the Roman victories proclaimed the greatness of the people among whom he came to take up his abode. No doubt the sight of these wonders excited the ardent spirit of Jerome, and made him resolve to achieve distinction also at the cost of toil and self-denial. He devoted himself to his studies with the utmost zeal, although he was not exempt from yielding also to the pleasures of that gay city, a weakness which he often afterwards bitterly lamented.

Among the amusements which the young students at Rome then favoured was that of writing burlesques, or satirical plays, in which they held up to ridicule their masters and other persons of note. Jerome has left us a curious specimen of one of these pieces. During the time that he spent at Rome, the heathen superstition, which had been almost overthrown by the Christian emperors, raised again its head for a short time under the apostate Emperor Julian, and Jerome saw the capitol reeking with the blood of numerous victims slain in honour of the false gods of pagan idolatry. But this senseless religion had no attractions for him. On the contrary, he determined now formally to enter into that Christian covenant for which he had been always destined, and at the age of twenty he was baptized into the Christian Church.

Eager to gain all information about that Christianity which had so long struggled in Rome against persecution and tyranny, Jerome now devoted himself to the examination of the Catacombs, those wonderful underground cavities which are so closely connected with the history of the early Christian Church.

" Under the city of Rome itself and under the plain on which it is built, for many miles there extend immense caverns, which form a second

Rome; august crypts sacred in the eyes of the Christian; the hiding-places and the first churches of the faithful in the days of persecution, and at length their last dwelling-places, where were deposited the mortal remains of the brethren, and of the Christian martyrs."*

" When I was young," says St. Jerome, "and was studying at Rome, I was wont with other youths of the same age and pursuits, to visit on the Lord's Days the tombs of the Apostles and Martyrs; and often to enter into those crypts which, sunk down into the depths of the earth, have, as you enter them, the bodies of the dead forming walls on either side of the passage, and are in such obscurity that almost the words of the prophet seem realised when he speaks of 'descending alive into the sepulchre.' At rare intervals light admitted from above tempers the horror of the darkness, but the openings are so small that you would rather account them as holes than as windows."†

In these hallowed caverns the Christians at Rome still worshipped, even after the time of

* Colombet, "Vie de St. Jérome," i. 47.
† Jerome, "Commentary on Ezekiel." This passage is still inscribed over the entrance to the catacombs at the church of St. Sebastian, in Rome.

persecution had ceased. They delighted to meet near the tomb of some famous martyr, whose remains had been deposited in the Catacombs, and calling to mind the great devotion which had been shown by him whose bones lay near them, to pledge themselves anew to the devout performance of their Christian duties.

Jerome, who was full of the ardent and fiery spirit which had supported the martyrs, could not have visited these scenes without being intensely moved by them. As yet, however, he was not in the practice of that strict and holy life to which he afterwards attained. He was still sometimes overborne by the temptations to pleasure and license, though he does not seem to have fallen into such excesses as Augustine did, and for which his penitence was so remarkable.

Having completed his studies at Rome, Jerome now determined to travel. Accompanied by a friend, named Bonosus, he visited much of France and Germany, and at the beautiful town of Trèves on the Moselle, he passed some time. For one eager to acquire knowledge, in those early days the labour of doing so was indeed severe. The rare copies of the works of great men must be transcribed by the hand, if they were to be possessed; they could not be easily bought at a moderate price as now. At Trèves we read of Jerome's copying the whole of Hilary's long treatise on Synods, as well as his Commentary on the Psalms; and here, removed from the temptations of Rome and occupied with sacred subjects, Jerome formed the serious resolution of henceforth dedicating himself strictly and entirely to the service of God. His friend Bonosus united with him in this determination.

After staying some time at Trèves, Jerome next went to Aquileia, then a city of great note and size, situated just at the head of the Adriatic. Here Jerome enjoyed the society of Christian friends of high mark and quality, one of the most distinguished of whom was Ruffinus the presbyter, a native of Aquileia, afterwards the devoted friend of Jerome, and then, when they differed on matters of doctrine, his fierce antagonist. Ruffinus was a man of great learning and patient study; he was also a person of the greatest devotion and piety. His desire to perfect himself in the devout life led him soon after this to quit Aquileia and Italy, and to make a journey to Egypt, to inspect for himself the way of living practised by the monks and solitaries in the deserts of Egypt, the fame of whose ascetic life was then spread throughout the Christian world. In his admiration for these recluses, and their hard and painful life, Jerome fully sympathised with him; in fact, there was no one of note among the Christians at that time who does not seem to have been carried away by admiration of these men, who practised the most strange austerities and vied with one another in the torments which they delighted to inflict upon their bodies. The great Athanasius, as was mentioned in his life, was a devout admirer of the hermits, and wrote the life of one of the most famous of them, named Anthony. Jerome also wrote the life of the hermit Paul, who was said to have passed some sixty or eighty years without seeing the face of man, living in a cavern where he was fed by ravens who brought him bread every evening. Anthony was reputed to hold converse with the wild beasts of the desert. Indeed, there was nothing too extravagant and absurd to be believed about these hermits, who were thought to be miracles of sanctity because they macerated their bodies, and leaving their fellow-Christians to all the dangers of a corrupt world, fled away to hide themselves in the desert.

Another remarkable person whose after history was much mixed up with that of St. Jerome, accompanied Ruffinus to Egypt out of the same admiration for the solitaries. This was Melania, a noble Roman lady, and a person of a most devout and charitable spirit. She was of one of the highest families in Rome and of great wealth. She had been married very young, and had gone through many trials, losing her children one after another, and at length her husband. On his death she determined to devote herself to a life of strict religious observance, and with this view she went to visit the far-famed Egyptian hermits. While sojourning among them she was most untiring and munificent in her deeds of charity, and was able to effect a very great kindness by redeeming some who had been seized and sold as slaves.

It is satisfactory, however, to know that neither Melania nor Ruffinus themselves adopted the hermit's life, and thus deprived the Church of their useful and energetic qualities. They both afterwards repaired to Jerusalem, where they founded and supported for many years most excellent and valuable institutions, viz.: places for rest and refreshment for the numerous pilgrims who made their way to the holy city to visit the spots which the Saviour of mankind had hallowed by His presence.

Nothing could exceed the terms of praise in which Jerome in after years extolled the good deeds of Melania, until he quarrelled with Ruffinus; and then, as Melania remained faithful to Ruffinus, he declared that she was as black as her name (in Greek, *Black*) and heaped the bitterest insults and reproaches upon her.

After passing some time at Aquileia, with the utmost profit and pleasure, Jerome once more visited Rome, but he did not long remain there. At this time he was tortured by a restlessness of spirit which allowed him no repose. His passions were strong and vehement, his devotion to religion was ardent, his thirst for learning excessive. He could not settle down quietly in any one spot or commence a regular course of life. He left Italy, and wandered on from place to place, through many lands, until at length he found himself at Antioch, the capital of Syria.

At Antioch, ever eager for study, and burning to acquire new knowledge, he became the disciple of Apollinarius, a man of beautiful character and the highest powers of mind, but who was unfortunately led into some errors of doctrine, which have thrown him into the list of heretics.

After remaining some time at Antioch, Jerome retired into the deserts of Syria, where he gave himself up to sacred study and the mortification of the flesh. At the same time he worked hard with his hands in tilling the ground, to provide himself with the necessary support and to keep mind and body in healthy condition. But with all this Jerome was far from being happy in this way of life. He could not command his thoughts, and often, in spite of his labours and mortifications, they would stray away to the pleasures of the gay capital of Rome. "Alas!" he cries, "how many times while imprisoned in this desert, and in that vast solitude which, scorched by the heat of the sun, affords for the monks only a fearful abode, did I think I was taking a part in the pleasures of Rome. Sitting alone, filled with bitterness, covered with a hideous garment, my skin burned to the colour of a negro, with none for my companions but scorpions and savage beasts, I seemed to be joining in the dance and revelry. Often did I pass day and night in uttering cries and beating my breast to regain, by the help of the Lord, my tranquillity. I wandered away into the desert, seeking the wildest mountains, the most precipitous rocks, for the place of my prayer, then sometimes did the Lord visit me and I seemed to be transported among the bands of angels."* Yet this period of his life was not unfruitful either to Jerome or to the Church. For it was now that he perfected himself in the Hebrew language, which he had long studied, and his profound knowledge of which afterwards enabled him to translate the whole Hebrew Bible into the Latin tongue. His diseased and excited state of body and mind led him to believe that at this time he had had a special vision, in which he seemed to be receiving chastisement from the hands of the Great Judge, for having paid too much attention to profane authors; and henceforth, as he wrote to Ruffinus, he had vowed to renounce every study but that of the Scriptures and Christian writings. Ruffinus did not fail to remind him afterwards that he had not kept his vow, for there is perhaps none of the Christian fathers whose writings abound so much with quotations and illustrations from the Classics as those of St. Jerome do.

About the year 379 or 380 Jerome was admitted to the order of Christian priesthood by Paul-

* St. Jerome, Letters.

inus, Bishop of Antioch. Of the dignity of this office Jerome held the very highest possible notions; but it is somewhat singular to discover that these notions of its dignity and responsibility should have prevented him from exercising one of its chief and most important functions, viz. that of celebrating the Holy Eucharist. This Jerome could not be induced to do, and afterwards, when he lived in the monastery at Bethlehem, the lay brethren were prevented from having this great means of Christian grace ministered to them, because he and Vincentius, another presbyter who lived with him and imitated his conduct, could not be brought to administer, out of their extreme humility.*

Jerome soon after this quitted Antioch, and still intent upon learning, repaired to Constantinople, with the intention of studying under that great orator and theologian, Gregory of Nazianzum. In the life of this father the circumstances under which he became archbishop of Constantinople have been fully detailed, as well as the wonderful work which he there performed in raising up the orthodox Church, which had been almost overpowered and stifled by the Arian

* Colombet, "Vie de St. Jérôme," i. 393.

heresy. It was always the pride and boast of Jerome that he had studied under one so distinguished as Gregory of Nazianzum, and had learned from his eloquent lips the great treasures of wisdom to be found in the Holy Scriptures. As a pupil of Gregory, Jerome must have been present in Constantinople at the meeting of the great Council there, which did so important a work by the additions which it made to the Creed of the Church. He witnessed the turning of the great body of bishops against St. Gregory, and the retirement of the latter from his high place. And when, in the following year, the Roman bishop desired to hold a Council with a special reference to the state of the Church of Antioch, which was distracted by divisions, Jerome, as one able to give the best information on the subject, was summoned to Rome to assist.

For a third time now did Jerome find himself in Rome; the place of his youthful studies, of his baptism, and of the many deep impressions which the ancient memorials of Christianity had excited in him. He was appointed to act as a secretary to the Council, and from his intimate knowledge of both the Eastern and Western Church, and his great learning and ability, no one could have

been more suited for the post. He remained at
Rome about three years, during which time he
wrote several of his works; but the most important
work which he performed was the revision of
the Latin translations of the New Testament,
which differed very much one from another, and
were often by no means true renderings of the
Greek original. Jerome removed from these
versions their chief faults, though he could not
leave them altogether in a satisfactory state.
He also revised the Latin Psalter, which was
made from the Greek translation of the Seventy
Interpreters. But these learned works were by
no means the whole employment of Jerome when
he was residing at Rome. At this time a very
remarkable movement was going on among the
noble and wealthy Roman ladies, many of whom
were desirous to devote themselves to the life of
strict religious observance in the monastic state.
This desire would seem not to have been generally
approved of by the clergy at Rome; but
Jerome, who held it to be the most acceptable
manner of pleasing God, eagerly upheld it, and
he was followed and almost besieged by those
ladies who desired instruction as to the religious
life. The most remarkable of these was Mar-

cella, a young widow of a noble Roman, who devoted herself to charitable works in company with some others of like spirit, and nearly thirty years after this time, when Rome was taken by the Goths, fell a victim to the cruelty of these barbarous invaders. There were also among these ladies a noble matron, named Paula, and her daughter Eustochium, who became the most devoted friends of Jerome. Paula had been the wife, for sixteen years, of a nobleman named Toxotius, and had borne him five children. On his death, struck with grief, she abandoned the world and divided the greater portion of her wealth among the poor. When some remonstrated with her that she was leaving no inheritance for her children, she replied that "she was leaving them the most precious inheritance which they could have, viz. the mercy of Jesus Christ." "It matters not," she said, "for me, if I be left destitute and have to beg my bread. There are many who would readily give alms to me, but this poor beggar who asks my help, if I should pass him by, might perhaps not meet with any one else to succour him."

We cannot but admire this spirit of Christian love, but when Paula, forgetting the claims which her family and position in life had upon her, would be satisfied with nothing less than entering the monastic state, we cannot think that her resolution was either wise or commendable. It must however be remembered that there was so much of open vice in the state of society at that time, especially perhaps at Rome, that we cannot altogether judge according to our modern standard. There were still great numbers who held to the religion of the old heathen false gods, still more perhaps who professed some form of philosophy without believing in any religion. Christianity had not as yet thoroughly penetrated throughout the whole population. Even those who professed themselves to be virgins devoted to religion, were often most reprehensible in their dress, manners, and conduct. Jerome, writing to Eustochium, the daughter of Paula, had to give her cautions and directions which seem indeed very strange to us, and which could only be justified by the gross corruption which was common in those days. The counsels of Jerome would perhaps have been better bestowed in teaching these ladies how to live holy Christian lives in the midst of this licentious society, and thus to leaven and improve it, than in encouraging them to shut themselves up in monasteries, and thus leave the world to its fate. But this short-sighted view of Christian duty was one from which scarcely any of the fathers of this age were exempt, and with Jerome the love of the monastic state and the life of asceticism was a perfect mania. It is impossible to deny that much that he wrote on this subject was senseless and puerile, if we are to describe it by no harsher name.

The letter of Jerome to Eustochium, in which he satirized bitterly the Christians of that day at Rome, and others of his fierce and cutting attacks, made him very much disliked at Rome. Ruffinus who, as we have seen, had been a great friend of Jerome, began now to oppose him. He says, " that the pagans and the enemies of God, the apostates, and the persecutors, all those who hated the Christian name, were eagerly transcribing this work of Jerome, because he had thrown the most shameful reproaches in it upon the whole body of Christians, and seemed to show that the charges made against the Christians by the Gentiles, and which they denied as falsities, were true; and that even worse things might be brought against them." Jerome had fallen into the error common to men of eager and over zealous temperament, of writing in an exaggerated strain, in order that he might more deeply impress. The excessive freedom and bitterness of his style was afterwards a subject of much regret to him. "When retired at Bethlehem," says one of his biographers, " he understood, when thinking over the past, that one has often cause for repentance for not having preserved silence."

Jerome determined now to quit Rome and the intrigues and troubles of life in a great city, and to retire to the Holy Land to live as a recluse given up to study and prayer. He was speedily followed by the widow Paula and her daughter Eustochium; for though the elder lady had several other children, she thought it profitable to leave them, that she might have the benefit of Jerome's counsels and religious instructions. They travelled together throughout Palestine, visiting with the utmost devotion all the places celebrated in the sacred history, and at length they determined to settle at Bethlehem, where Jerome was to occupy a small building, living as a hermit, and Paula was to found a religious establishment which should have for its especial work to attend to the wants of the numerous pilgrims who visited the place of the Saviour's birth.

Jerome in his letters gives a beautiful description of the calm and religious peace which reigned at Bethlehem. "Here," he says, "in the city of Christ all is simple and country-like. The profound silence is only broken by the singing of psalms. On all sides one may hear the labourer who, driving his cart, sings the Alleluiah. The mower, exhausted with his toil, refreshes himself by the singing of psalms; the vinedresser, cutting his vine with his crooked knife, chants some hymn of David. These are the songs of the country, these are the love-ditties. These take the place of the whistling of the shepherd, these are the very tools of the labourer."

The special work to which Jerome now devoted himself was the commenting upon the Epistles of St. Paul; but at Bethlehem he soon found that he suffered great interruptions in his studies from the number of pilgrims who came there. All of these desired to make the acquaintance of one who had now become famous for his learning and piety, and to get some instruction from him. By degrees the narrow cell in which he had first established himself was exchanged for a large monastery, built partly at the expense of Paula and partly at his own expense, the lands and houses which he had inherited in Dalmatia being sold for that purpose. Although the numerous visitors to this religious house were not conducive to his sacred employments, Jerome nevertheless thought it his duty to receive all with hospitality. "Hospitality," he says, "is cherished in our hearts in the monastery, and with joyous front and all civility we receive those who come to us; for we fear lest Mary coming with Joseph should not find where to shelter herself, and lest Jesus, in a manner rejected, should say to us, 'I was a stranger, and ye took me not in.' There is no hour, no moment, in which we do not receive crowds of monks. The solitude of our monastery is changed into a perpetual swarm of guests."*

The adjoining monastery, in which Paula presided over a large body of nuns, was kept closely secured, and the great burden of entertaining the pilgrims was thrown upon Jerome. But, in spite of all the interruptions, the work which he performed at this period for the eluci-

* Jerome, "Preface to Ezekiel."

dation of the Holy Scriptures was enormous. "More than any other father of the Church," says his biographer, "did he watch over the sacred deposit of the Scriptures, the foundation of our faith, and open the sacred path of the true explanation of them. Noble and glorious title, which shall never cease in the eyes of Christians to add brilliant flowers to his holy crown." *

Jerome translated into Latin, or revised the translation of the whole of the Old Testament from the original Hebrew, and in his Prefaces and Commentaries on various books did very much towards the explanation of the sacred writings. The translation which he made is the foundation of the Latin version of the Bible, now most commonly known under the name of the Vulgate or common version; but it is not altogether represented by the Vulgate. The work of some more ignorant translators than Jerome has found a place in this, so that the Latin Vulgate contains many inaccuracies and errors, and is not to be compared for value to our English version made under King James I. Considering the great amount of ignorance in which the Latin Church

* Colombet, "Vie de St. Jérôme," ii. 67.

must have been as to the Scriptures before the time of Jerome, having only bad translations of the Greek Translation of the Seventy, we cannot but ascribe to him the greatest credit for the valuable work which he performed, at the cost of so much labour, for the instruction of his fellow-Christians.

Of all the writings of Jerome at this period it is impossible to speak in the same terms of praise. He wrote against Jovinian, whose opinions for the most part are such as would be held orthodox by members of the Church of England; and in his treatise he spoke so bitterly against the married state, that some of his own chief friends endeavoured to suppress the work. Vigilantius, a presbyter of France, had made a manly and Christian protest against the excessive reverence beginning now to be shown towards the relics of departed Saints, holy places and things. This, as he pointed out, was leading to idolatry, and on that account ought to be guarded against and checked. He also, like Jovinian, declared that there was no special virtue in the single life, and that a virtuous married state was equal or superior. These sentiments, in which Vigilantius displayed his true understanding of the Scriptures, drew upon him the wrath of Jerome, who assailed him in his usual violent style.

It was unfortunate that, whenever he was involved in controversy, Jerome seems to have forgotten all Christian gentleness and meekness, and to have railed and scolded without measure or restraint. Thus, though there is much which we owe to Jerome, and many points in which he deserves our admiration, there is also much in his views which cannot easily be defended. But it must not be forgotten that Jerome lived at a most critical time in the history of the Church. After the Roman Emperors had become Christian and Christianity had been made the religion of the State, a vast flood of corruption, drawn from the relics of the old heathenism and superstition, entered the Church. So corrupt was the state of society, that it may have been in some cases absolutely necessary for the preservation of religion that the ascetic and cloistral life should have been encouraged. Jerome's fault appears to have been that he made that which was good "for the present distress" of universal application, and that he not only wrote it up as the higher state, but also spoke most bitterly and satirically of every other state. With him the mortification of the body seems to be the one high and surpassing virtue.

Doubtless Christians had a difficult path to tread in the fourth century. The worst forms of heresy were everywhere prevalent, and constant wars, tumults, and bloodshed shook society to its foundations. How terrible is the picture which Jerome himself draws:—" My spirit shudders at the task of painting the ruins of our time. For more than twenty years Roman blood has been poured out day by day between Constantinople and the Julian Alps. The empire is the prey of the barbarians, who devastate, tear and plunder it. How many matrons and virgins of God, how many noble and pure bodies have been the plaything of these savage beasts. Bishops made slaves, priests murdered, churches overthrown, horses stabled at the altars of Christ, the relics of martyrs dug up! Everywhere there is woe, everywhere are there groans, and the abundant image of death." *

In the contemplation of these terrible disorders Jerome might well congratulate himself on his tranquil retreat at Bethlehem. But even here disturbances, though of another character,

* Jerome's Letters.

were not wanting. The fiery monk had become involved in a quarrel with John, Bishop of Jerusalem, and in this quarrel he seems not to have been free from blame. He had allowed another bishop, who had no jurisdiction in the diocese of Jerusalem, to ordain his brother Paulinian as a priest for the monastery; and he now pretended to consider that his monastery was exempt from episcopal control, though there does not seem any good reason why it should have been. There were also other subjects of quarrel. Jerome had once been a great admirer of the writings of Origen, a very learned Alexandrian doctor, who had done much for the explanation of the Scriptures, but had also fallen into many strange errors. The Bishop of Jerusalem was also an admirer of the same great writer. But Jerome had now been shown the dangerous nature of the teaching of Origen, and had declared against him, while Bishop John still held with him. This change in Jerome's views produced also a fierce quarrel between him and his former friend Ruffinus.

Ruffinus and Melania, whose settling at Jerusalem was before mentioned, had continued there ever since, gaining the love and respect of the whole Christian world by their charitable deeds towards the pilgrims. The friendship between Jerome and Ruffinus had been somewhat interrupted, but now when Ruffinus published a translation of the chief treatise of Origen, and in his preface quoted the words which Jerome had formerly used of Origen, calling him the greatest of Christian doctors, and second only to the Apostles, Jerome's wrath against him knew no bounds. Ruffinus had left Jerusalem for Italy, and published his version of Origen there; Jerome therefore despatched after him a justification of himself, for ever having favoured the tenets of Origen. This is not a very commendable production, as the chief point urged by Jerome, is that the love of Origen was an error of his youth, which his mature years corrected, whereas the fact is that he had never in any way shown his condemnation of the tenets of Origen until he was sixty years of age.

We turn readily from these disputes to a beautiful picture of devoted Christian virtue, which the life and writings of Jerome put before us. Among the most noble matrons of Rome, the descendant of the famous Fabius, who had saved the State from Hannibal, was Fabiola, the wife of a man who was unworthy of her, and who, by his gross licentiousness, gave her, as she considered, a legal justification in seeking for a divorce. This she obtained, and then being free by the law of Rome to marry again, she took a second husband, who died not long after their marriage. His death appears to have touched Fabiola, not only with sorrow, but with deep self-reproach for having entered on a second marriage. Possessed of great wealth, and admired for her beauty and acquirements, she now determined to forsake all worldly pleasure, and to give herself up to good works. On Easter Eve the bishop and priests of Rome, going to the service at the great church of St. John Lateran, observed a woman covered with the coarsest garments of penitence, and showing such an overwhelming sorrow, that none could see her without being moved. Being brought by the bishop into the Church, she was found to be no other than Fabiola, so well known among the noblest of Rome. The work that she now commenced is worthy of all attention, inasmuch as she was the foundress of the first hospital which was built in Rome, that peculiarly Christian institution, which no heathen nation had cared to

FABIOLA ASSISTING THE SICK.—*Page* 231.

build, and which up to this period appears to have been almost unknown in the Christian Church.

In the work that Fabiola now undertook, we see the true devotion of the Christian, the perfect following of the footsteps of Christ. She did not shut herself up, occupied only with herself, as some of the other ladies highly commended by Jerome had done. On the contrary, she forgot herself; she sacrificed her ease, her fastidiousness, her repose to ministering to the pressing wants of her fellow-Christians. Having built and endowed a hospital, she sought out and conveyed thither with her own hands, often carrying in her arms, the most grievous and destitute sufferers from every quarter of the city. The maimed, the fever-stricken, those suffering from frightful sores, and the most repulsive forms of ailment, this delicate lady, a true sister of charity, tended with devoted care. Nor did she confine herself to the aid of the sick. Every form of poverty and want she alleviated by her wealth, and not alone in Rome, but throughout Italy her good works were known. After long devotion to these labours, Fabiola was possessed with an eager desire to visit the Holy Land, and she passed some time at the religious house at Bethlehem, where her hearty zeal for instruction in the Scriptures corresponded with her earnest labours of charity. On her return to Italy she built another hospital at the port of Rome, at the mouth of the Tiber, as Rome ever attracted to it numerous pilgrims from all parts of the world, and many of these arrived at the end of their voyage destitute and suffering. Soon after this was accomplished this devout lady died, and all Rome strove to do honour to her funeral. The funeral oration which Jerome composed on her holy life and works of Christian love was the most enduring monument she could receive.

Jerome was now brought into correspondence with St. Augustine, the famous Bishop of Hippo, in Africa, who was much interested in Jerome's labours for the explanation of the Scriptures. He had occasion to find fault with Jerome's interpretations of that passage in the Epistle to the Galatians where the Apostle Paul says that he "withstood St. Peter to the face because he was to be blamed."* Jerome had explained this as meaning that St. Paul did not really find fault with St. Peter, but only appeared to do so on account of the Gentile converts. Augustine rightly condemned this interpretation

* Galatians ii. 11.

as "overthrowing the truth and the authority of the Scripture," if words were not to be taken in their plain and obvious meaning. Upon this point some dispute arose between these two great men, but it was soon terminated, and they continued afterwards to feel and express the highest respect for one another.

From his retreat at Bethlehem the watchful and vigorous Christian teacher maintained a close observation of all the events which affected the Church, and bitter indeed must have been his feelings at marking the evils which were at that period pressing heavy upon Christendom. The Roman empire of the West was now tottering to its fall. Effeminacy, vice and dissipation reigned almost unchecked in the great capital city of Rome; the Emperors were weak and powerless, while great bodies of fierce barbarians from the north were threatening the very existence of the empire. Those from whom there was now the most pressing danger were the Ostrogoths, who, coming from the countries around the Black Sea, had already made several incursions into Europe, under Alaric, their warlike king. These Goths had been converted to Christianity, but their religion had taken the form of Arianism, and it had not done much to soften their manners or to make them abandon those fierce and cruel habits to which they were naturally inclined. In the year 408 they entered Italy and besieged Rome, but they were then bought off by an enormous ransom. Very soon after they appeared again, and the Roman Emperor, who dwelt at Ravenna, being utterly unable to withstand them, they captured the famous city (Aug. 24, 410). For a whole week the unfortunate Romans were delivered over to massacre, pillage, and outrage. Every horror which war brings with it was heaped upon them. The Goths were eager and insatiable spoilers, and having no regard for any of the beautiful treasures of art which Rome contained, they did on all sides irreparable damage. Meantime immense numbers of the more distinguished citizens escaped with their families into Africa and the East, and the charity of the Christians in those lands was taxed to the uttermost to save them from utter annihilation.

When Jerome heard of the capture of Rome, he was so overcome by the news, that he remained for some time almost stupefied, and, as he said, had forgotten even his own name. He was then occupied with his Commentary on

Ezekiel, and in the preface to the Third Book we find him saying, "Who indeed could have believed that Rome, elevated by her victories to the head of the whole world, would be overthrown; that she would become the tomb of the people whom she had produced; that all the countries of the East, Egypt and Africa, would be filled with a crowd of slaves and servants from this city so long dominant; that holy Bethlehem would receive each day mendicants of either sex who once were nobles, overflowing with all sorts of riches? Unable as we are to succour them, we still compassionate their lot—we join our tears to theirs. We cannot see them coming in crowds without groaning; we have therefore suspended our studies, desiring rather to act Scripture than to write it, to do rather than to say holy things."

The unfortunate fugitives from Rome added greatly to that crowd of visitors of which Jerome so often complains as bringing great distraction to his studies; yet with untiring energy, though now in extreme old age, he laboured at his work, and succeeded in writing valuable commentaries on almost the whole of the Prophets. In addition to these Scriptural studies, he was also now involved in controversy with another set of opinions which began greatly to spread in the Church. These were the doctrines taught by Pelagius, a monk born in Britain, who maintained that the sin of Adam did not affect the human race in the way of making them naturally corrupt, but only by putting sin in their way, which they would be inclined to practise, and by bringing in death as the punishment of sin. He also held that man might reach a state of sinlessness or perfection in this life. There was much in the teaching of Pelagius which was false and dangerous, and both Augustine and Jerome wrote several treatises against it; but John, Bishop of Jerusalem, was inclined to favour Pelagius, and at a synod held at Diospolis he was acquitted of heresy and pronounced orthodox. This decision, however, was due to a mistake, and the fact that Greek bishops did not fully understand the terms of a Latin heresy. The only effect which it had upon Jerome was to make him denounce the Pelagians more violently; and so exasperated did they become against him, that they went in a large body to Bethlehem, and attacked the monastery where Jerome lived. He escaped with great difficulty from their hands, as did also Eustochium, who had lived for so many years in the closest Christian friendship with him. Jerome took refuge in a fortified town, and appealed to the Roman bishop for his influence and aid to protect him.

But though his bitter and fierce manner of writing and speaking had stirred up against him such violent enemies, Jerome never for a moment relaxed it, and some of the most severe things which he wrote were penned at this time. His zeal ever prompted him to fight what he considered to be the battles of the Church, and in fighting them he spared none, and thus exhibited more zeal than charity. At length, worn out by ceaseless toil and great age, he died at Bethlehem of a fever, in the year 420, and in the 75th year of his age.

We have endeavoured to show the points in which this great Christian doctor seems to be not deserving of praise, but we must not forget the entire and burning devotion with which he gave his life and his great talents to the cause of religion; the loving care with which he ministered to those numerous Christian friends who sought his counsels and instruction; the zeal which led him to labour so abundantly in the translation and explanation of the Holy Scriptures, and the immense debt of gratitude which the Christian Church owes him for this devoted and holy toil.

ST. JOHN CHRYSOSTOM.

JOHN, called Chrysostom, or the Golden-mouthed, from his wonderful powers of oratory, was born at Antioch, the capital of Syria, about the year 347. There is perhaps not one of all the Christian fathers whose life and works we can dwell upon with such unmixed pleasure and profit as we do upon those of this holy and zealous man and unrivalled Christian preacher. Placed as he was in a most difficult position, and having to contend against the grossest licentiousness and corruption in the court and capital, he bore a faithful witness for virtue and truth in spite of fierce persecution, and he has left to the Church a sacred treasure in his writings and expositions of Holy Scripture. His father Secundus was a general in the imperial army, and his mother Anthusa was left a widow soon after his birth. He had one sister, a little younger than himself. His mother was a woman of very religious character, and from his earliest youth

John seems to have been devoted to piety and virtue. He was educated at Antioch, and instruction in oratory, in which he afterwards became so celebrated, was given to him by Libanius, the same famous heathen orator, who had also instructed St. Basil.

Of John's powers Libanius had the highest opinion, and he used to declare that he of all his pupils was the fittest to succeed him in his office of teacher of Rhetoric, had not, as he said, " the Christians stolen him from us." It was happy for the Christian Church that the talented young man had been thus " stolen," and that his great powers were to be dedicated to the cause of Christian truth. His chief teacher in religious knowledge was Diodorus, afterwards Bishop of Tarsus, and from him John is thought to have learned his peculiar manner of interpreting the Scriptures. Before his time Christian interpreters were too much taken up in trying to find out an allegorical sense of the Divine Word; but Chrysostom introduced the method of interpreting it grammatically and according to its plain meaning, and on this meaning founding practical applications to virtue and godliness. His eager desire for learning the Scriptures was so intense, that he had formed a scheme with a young friend to retire into solitude to devote themselves entirely to this work; but from this he was dissuaded by his mother, who did not wish to be thus deserted by him. Afterwards, however, he appears to have carried out his project and retired into the mountains in the neighbourhood of Antioch, where for some years he dwelt in the cell of an aged hermit, intensely occupied in his studies. He is said to have committed the whole of the Scriptures to memory. At length, feeling himself qualified for Christian work by which others might be benefited, he returned to Antioch, and was ordained deacon by Meletius, the bishop of that see. Five years he remained in this office, during which time he composed several books, one on the duties of the priesthood—which has always been held to be a most valuable work—and another on Divine Providence. He was then ordained priest, and on this occasion preached his first sermon, which was full of humble expressions about himself and his unfitness for so holy an office, though it would have been difficult to find any one who was more excellently fitted for it.

At once he seems to have become the most

admired and popular preacher of the city, and the sad circumstances which soon took place at Antioch gave a peculiar significance to his sermons, and raised him to the highest fame. A heavy and oppressive tax had been laid upon that great city by Theodosius the Emperor, and so exasperated were the people of Antioch at this, that they rose in tumult, and having driven out the government officers, threw down the statues of the Emperor and the royal family, and tying ropes to their feet dragged them in derision throughout the city. The Emperor hearing of this was terribly enraged, and prepared to take fearful vengeance upon Antioch. He sent his commissioners, accompanied by a large armed force, and the people of Antioch, now greatly alarmed, expected no less than death or banishment for their rebellion. In their terror they sought consolation in religious services; the churches were thronged, and the sermons of the Christian ministers, especially those of Chrysostom, were listened to with the most eager attention. The discourses which Chrysostom delivered on this occasion have come down to us under the name of "Homilies on the Statues." They were delivered in the time of Lent and in the midst of the terror which the punishments threatened by the Emperor caused, and they produced a wonderful effect. "Many who had never been within the church doors, but spent their whole time at the theatres, now fled to the church as a common sanctuary, and there stayed from morning until night. You could scarce hear anything but weeping and mourning, prayers and tears; and peculiar litanies were framed on purpose, and hymns of lamentation, to solicit Heaven that God would dispose the heart of the Emperor to clemency and compassion towards them."*

The Emperor's judges on their arrival proceeded to inflict severe punishment on the city. All public places were shut up, all trade stopped; guards were posted in every place, and all the chief citizens were arrested and examined, one by one, to discover if they had any share in the revolt, and those that were convicted were scourged and imprisoned. In the meantime Flavian, the aged Bishop of Antioch, had been making his way to Constantinople to solicit, in humble guise, the clemency of the Emperor. Theodosius, who, though subject to violent passions, was a good

* Cave, "Life of St. Chrysostom."

and a religious prince, received him kindly, and at once granted the pardon of the people of Antioch, sending back the bishop with all haste to declare it. On his return with the welcome pardon he was received with the greatest joy at Antioch, and Chrysostom, as the most famous preacher of the city, was appointed to deliver an oration of welcome and of thanks to him for the valuable services he had rendered to his city.

The love and admiration which the people of Antioch felt towards Chrysostom now knew no bounds. They were proud of his powers and of his fame as a preacher, and they were apprehensive lest by being promoted to some higher dignity he should be taken from them. This promotion was soon to come. In the year 397 Nectarius, Bishop of Constantinople, who, it will be remembered, succeeded Gregory of Nazianzum, died, and Arcadius, who was now the Emperor, sought to find some distinguished man to fill the high post of archbishop of the Imperial city, and second prelate in rank of all the Christian world. His minister Eutropius, who had known Chrysostom at Antioch, at once recommended him for the place, and the Emperor consented. But a difficulty arose in carrying out the appointment. It was known that the people of Antioch would not part with their favourite preacher without raising a tumult, and so Asterius, the governor, who was entrusted with the execution of the Emperor's orders, was obliged to resort to artifice. Pretending some private business with Chrysostom, he induced him to accompany him in his chariot the first stage out of Antioch. Here officers of the Emperor were waiting, and to these he delivered up Chrysostom, who was forced in spite of himself to accompany them to Constantinople. But though he was brought almost like a prisoner, he was received at Constantinople with all joy and triumph. The Emperor paid him every honour, and summoned a synod of the most eminent bishops for his consecration and introduction to his office.

Chrysostom, thus placed without his own seeking in this important and responsible situation, began at once to enter upon its duties with great vigour. Many abuses had grown up in the Church of Constantinople during the time of his predecessor. A custom had become very general for the clergy to have women living in their houses as housekeepers, which, although it might have been done innocently, yet caused much scandal in that profligate city. The clergy had also become much noted for their luxury and their fondness of attending at the banquets of the great; and in order to give themselves more freedom, had almost disused the late services wont to be held in the churches, and which were most convenient for the attendance of the laity. All these irregularities the new bishop at once violently attacked. It may be that he used too little prudence and moderation in his censures, but the effect of them was to exasperate the clergy greatly against him, while at the same time he was strongly supported by the laity, who were much taken by his preaching and the holy sincerity which his conduct showed. For Chrysostom had no notion of imposing strict discipline upon the clergy, while he himself lived luxuriously. The banquets and pomp which had been prevalent at the episcopal palace he at once disused. A great part of the revenues of the see was given over to found hospitals for the infirm and sick, over which he appointed some of his clergy to preside, that they might give a religious character to the life of the inmates. Nor, as he reformed his own household, and sought to reform the clergy, did he stop there, but he also sought to improve, by Christian reproof and discipline, the lax manners and vicious lives of the great and rich at Constantinople. The eloquent sermons which he directed against their licentious lives remain to us to attest his zeal and eloquence and fearlessness, but there were many powerful persons who felt themselves severely condemned, and who were bitterly indignant against the great Christian preacher.

It was evident that one who, like Chrysostom, did not fear the face of man when in the discharge of his duty, would always have many enemies to contend against. Eutropius, the Emperor's favourite, who had been the means of bringing Chrysostom to Constantinople, felt among others the weight of his censures for his cruelty and debauchery. But soon the good bishop was able to show that it was the man's sins and not his person which he condemned. Disgrace, which usually falls to the lot of the over-favoured ministers of kings at some time or other, overtook Eutropius. His life was threatened by an armed crowd, whom he had angered by his tyranny, and he was obliged to fly for shelter into the church of the archbishop. Now the right which was claimed by accused persons of finding asylum in churches was one of the very rights which Eutropius himself had often violated, and the angry mob would have retaliated upon him, by tearing him out of the church, had not Chrysostom risen and in an eloquent oration claimed their forbearance on the Christian ground of returning good for evil. Such power had he over his hearers, that he was able to persuade them to lay aside their evil passions and to suffer the disgraced favourite to leave the city in peace.

In the next event of his life which is recorded we are not sure that Chrysostom is so much to be commended as in this last. Gainas, a Gothic general, had risen to great power and distinction in the Emperor's army, and, being an Arian, he had made a demand to the Emperor that he and his countrymen should be allowed one of the churches in Constantinople in which they might worship. Chrysostom persuaded the Emperor to refuse this request, and he was so far right, as there was a law of the Emperor Theodosius which prohibited the concession. But he does not seem to have been prudent or decorous in speaking so tauntingly and bitterly to Gainas in presence of the Emperor as he did, and when the Goth was driven into rebellion by the treatment he received, and his countrymen in Constantinople were attacked, and (to the number of 7,000, it is said) took sanctuary in a church, we do not find that the archbishop interfered to save them. On the contrary, the Goths were deliberately massacred, by men who were too cowardly to meet them in fair fight, by having burning pieces of wood thrown down upon them from the roof. We should have been glad to find it recorded that the archbishop tried to stop this butchery; but, though it is possible he may have done so, we have no proof of it.

There must have been something fine and noble about the character of Gainas; for when, shortly after this, Chrysostom undertook an embassy to him—a service manifestly of great danger to the archbishop—he received him most courteously, and treated him with the highest honour.

The work of Chrysostom at Constantinople was not confined to his own city and diocese. Being the principal bishop of a large division of the Church, many appeals and complaints were brought to him, which he had to hear and settle. Very gross disorders prevailed in the Eastern Church at that time. Simony, or the selling of orders for money, was not uncommon, and there was much treachery and ill-feeling among the bishops one against another. Wherever it was practicable, Chrysostom removed these scandals, and his own high reputation for piety and virtue enabled him to do much.

The Arians, though not allowed to have a church within the walls of the city, nevertheless annoyed the orthodox Christians by going in procession through the streets, singing hymns, and then repairing to their church outside the walls. Chrysostom, in order to counteract the influence which they might thus gain over the common people, introduced the custom of solemn processions of the clergy and chief members of the Church, who chanted litanies and hymns. This custom led to some serious disturbances, but it was nevertheless continued, and has remained as a favourite religious service in many parts of the Church up to the present day.

The zeal with which Chrysostom reproved abuses wherever he found them, soon stirred up enemies in Constantinople, who were both willing and able to injure him. The chief of these was the Empress Eudoxia, a woman of vicious character, who completely influenced her husband, the

Emperor Arcadius. Chrysostom had preached a sermon, in which he was thought to have compared her to Jezebel, who entertained the false priests at her table; and Eudoxia, bitterly enraged against him, determined to be revenged. For this purpose she brought to Constantinople Theophilus, Patriarch of Alexandria, an ancient enemy of Chrysostom, who gathered a synod of about forty bishops at a country-house near Constantinople, called, from a famous oak-tree near it, "The Oak;" on which account this synod is usually termed the Synod of the Oak. It was altogether against the rule of the Church for this synod to proceed against one in the position of Chrysostom, but it was supported by the power of the State, and though the accusations brought against Chrysostom were absurd as well as untrue, it decreed that he should be deposed from his office and banished. The people on hearing this were greatly excited, and would have defended their beloved bishop at any cost, but the good prelate would not encourage them to put themselves in peril for his sake, and yielding to his persecutors, he was carried away by a band of soldiers, and sent to Hieron, a place on the Black Sea.

His banishment was the signal for terrible tumults to break out in the city. Although the Court party and the great ladies were against him, yet the majority of the citizens were truly attached to him. Many of the clergy shut up their churches and refused to officiate while their bishop was in exile. Some of these were attacked and put to death by the Emperor's soldiers, and so fierce was the tumult, that the Empress and her friends were in dismay. In the midst of this there happened one of those great convulsions of nature which are apt to strike terror into men's minds, even when their consciences do not accuse them of wrong, as they must have done in this case. A terrible earthquake spread ruin and destruction through the city. The Empress at once sent messengers eagerly to solicit the return of the banished bishop, and to declare that she had had no hand in his banishment. Although Chrysostom must have known this to be untrue, yet for the sake of the Church he was willing to return, although he refused to enter the city until he had been formally cleared of the charges made against him by a greater synod than that which had condemned him. The Empress, however, seeing the eagerness of the people, by the most exaggerated expressions of her joy at his return, prevailed on him to yield, and he was conducted on his way by crowds, who sang hymns composed for the occasion, carrying torches in their hands, and in this triumphant manner conducted him to his cathedral; nor would they be satisfied until Chrysostom had ascended the pulpit and made an oration to them. A synod of about sixty bishops was now brought together, which reversed the sentence which had been passed against Chrysostom, and entirely acquitted him of all fault.

The good bishop might seem to be now fairly restored to his former high position; but the calm did not last long. Soon after his return a silver statue was erected to the Empress Eudoxia, close to the great church of St. Sophia, where Chrysostom ministered. Around this statue all sorts of disorderly festivities and games used to take place, to the great annoyance of those who worshipped in the cathedral. Chrysostom spoke very sharply of these things, and of the Empress herself, who encouraged them. Hearing of this, Eudoxia was again enraged, and the bishop, who did not combine prudence with his zeal, preaching in his church on the history of John the Baptist, said, " Now again Herodias raves and is vexed, again she dances, again she seeks to have John the Baptist's head in a charger. Again Jezebel goes up and down trying how she may ravish away Naboth's vineyard and drive holy Elias into the wilderness." These expressions were of course immediately conveyed to the Empress, who at once prepared to revenge herself for the insult.

On account of Chrysostom's great popularity, it was necessary for her to proceed with caution, and it was not until the Easter after his return that the plans of his enemies were put into execution. At that time the Emperor's warrant that Chrysostom should again depart into exile was signed, and immediately the soldiers began to use the most violent and barbarous measures against all those who adhered to him, so that the holy festival of Easter was troubled with tumults and general sadness. The friends and followers of the bishop were plundered, imprisoned, and even killed; he himself was kept a prisoner within his own house, until he could be conveyed away with safety.

When at length the Emperor's warrant for his removal was sent to him, the holy man exclaimed to the bishops who were with him, " Come, let us go to pray, and join our forces with the guardian angels of the Church." He then entered the church, and after paying his devotions, took a tender and Christian farewell of all who were with him there, departing secretly, in order to avoid an outbreak of the people. A large crowd, hearing that Chrysostom was in the church, was waiting at the door to receive him, and at length growing impatient, a party went into the church to look for him. Upon these the doors were shut by the soldiers, who wished to take them prisoners, and their friends outside finding this, rushed against the door of the church and forced it open. In the disturbance which followed a fire somehow broke out in the church, and rapidly spreading, it consumed the whole of the magnificent building, as well as the Senate House, which stood next to it, destroying many precious monuments of ancient art.

While this disturbance was raging, the good bishop was being conveyed away to his undeserved banishment, and the see being declared vacant, Arsacius, the brother of Nectarius, the former bishop, was appointed to occupy it. A most severe decree was now put forth against those who should remain faithful to Chrysostom; for the greater part of the people refused to communicate with the new bishop, or to let him have authority in their churches. The soldiers attacked them in their assemblies with violence, tortured and ill-treated them, not sparing even the women, if they would not abandon the cause of Chrysostom.

Among those who suffered much at their hands was Olympias, a noble lady specially devoted to Chrysostom, and to whom he wrote a large number of letters, which are still preserved. She was a person of noble birth, great wealth, and remarkable beauty, and was married early to Nebridius, who was a governor of a province under the Emperor. Her husband was put to death by the Emperor on the accusation of treason about two years after their marriage, and Olympias determined now to devote herself to a life of Christian good works, refusing all offers of a second marriage. Accordingly she was made a deaconess of the Church at Constantinople, and distributing all her money to the poor and for the service of the Church, she employed herself in the ministrations belonging to her office. To Chrysostom she was devotedly attached, and usually waited on him as a servant, as was the custom for deaconesses to do for the bishops. Stedfastly refusing on his banishment to turn against him, she too was banished; but in her exile, mindful of the bishop's necessities, she supplied him with money and other needful help.

Meanwhile the good bishop was being conveyed by the Emperor's officers to a place called Cucusus, on the borders of Armenia, a place of a cold climate and barren soil, and in the midst of a wild and half-heathen population. He suffered much on his journey from weakness and sickness, but he met with some kind friends, who out of respect for his high character and office gladly ministered to his wants. At Cæsarea in Cappadocia he was very badly treated, through the jealousy of the bishop of that place, who stirred up the monks to attack and annoy him. He was compelled to depart suddenly in the middle of the night, and travelling in the darkness, the mule on which he rode fell with him and endangered his life. He spent two months on his painful journey, suffering both in body and mind, but the constant respect and kindness with which he was received by all good church people cheered his spirit. At one place a company of friends came to meet him, who exclaimed one to another,

"It were better the sun should not shine in the firmament than that John should be silenced." At Cucusus also, the place of his banishment, he was most kindly received by the people, who waited zealously upon him, supplying him with provisions and with all that he needed. The great men of the country were also eager in their attentions, and the bishop of the see was so bent to do him honour, that he offered to resign his see in order that Chrysostom might occupy it. His health also rapidly improved, from the cold and bracing air of the place. Thus were the afflictions which the malice of men had heaped upon this holy bishop turned by a merciful Providence into blessings.

The very day after his arrival, one of his deaconesses from Constantinople, an aged lady named Sabiniana, came to Cucusus, having boldly encountered all the fatigues of the journey that she might still minister to her beloved bishop Constantius, also one of his favourite presbyters, came to join him.

Chrysostom, whose zeal did not for a moment slacken because his place of abode was changed, occupied himself busily in teaching and preaching, and by means of funds which he received from Olympias and others, was able to confer many temporal benefits on those among whom he lived. A marauding tribe called the Isaurians, who lived in the mountains of Taurus, had carried away many of the people of Cucusus, whom they treated as slaves. Many of these Chrysostom now redeemed, and restored them to their friends. He also vigorously prosecuted schemes for the spread of Christianity among those nations which had not as yet fully received it. One of these was the Goths, who were afterwards destined to work so great a destruction in the empire of the West. Chrysostom had consecrated Unilas, a Goth, to be a bishop, when he was still at Constantinople, and had sent him among his countrymen, where he had had great success in preaching the gospel. He had now sent to beg for some assistants to be forwarded to him, and Chrysostom, hearing that the messengers had gone to Constantinople, wrote to Olympias to beg her to procure their being sent to him, for that he desired especially to further this matter.

Besides these active and useful employments, Chrysostom at this time wrote several books and a vast number of letters to the many faithful who desired communication with him, looking up to him as they did as the most distinguished Christian bishop then alive in the world. To the clergy who had been imprisoned or ill-treated on his account he wrote most kind and consoling epistles, bidding them to be constant for the sake of the truth and to rejoice when they suffered for righteousness' sake. While thus occupied in his retreat, the unhappy Church at Constantinople suffered all sorts of persecution at the hands of the usurping bishop, who could not forgive the people for being still attached to their lawful pastors.

The whole Christian world now felt the scandal which was brought on the Christian name by the undeserved banishment of so great a man as Chrysostom. The Emperor of the West and the Bishop of Rome took active steps to obtain the opinion of a General Council on his case, but the arts of the Empress Eudoxia and of those now in power at Constantinople foiled them. Meantime the abode of Chrysostom at Cucusus became dangerous from the continued inroads of the Isaurians into the territory, so that he was removed to Arabissus, a city of the Lesser Armenia, for greater safety. Here he was exposed to many hardships, which brought on him a long and dangerous illness, yet whenever he was able, he ceased not to preach to the rude people of the country.

About this time he wrote to Innocent, Bishop of Rome, a letter, in which he says: "I am now in the third year of my banishment, exposed to famine, pestilence, war, continual sieges, to an incredible solitude and desolation, to death every day, and to the points of the Isaurian swords." Still Chrysostom's enemies were not satisfied, but finding that he secured wherever he went the love and care of those around him, they designed to remove him to a still worse place. He was now ordered to be conveyed to a town called Pityus, in the neighbourhood of the Black Sea, a place remarkable for its desolate and miserable condition. The soldiers who conveyed him treated him very roughly, and appeared to try to increase the fatigues and trials of the journey by ill-usage. The enfeebled health of the bishop completely broke down under these hardships. The soldiers, finding him too ill to proceed, conveyed him into a little chapel or oratory, which they passed on their way. Here the good bishop, rapidly sinking, received the Holy Eucharist, and having made his last prayer, and concluded with his usual doxology, "Glory be to God for all things that happen," he meekly and quietly resigned his soul to his Saviour. This was in the year 407 A.D., and in the fifty-second year of the age of Chrysostom. Thus early did the persecuting violence of evil men, together with his own burning zeal and laborious devotion, extinguish one of the most brilliant lights which has ever shone in the Church of Christ.

ST. AUGUSTINE.

Augustine, the most famous of all the Fathers of the Church, and who has exercised a greater influence over Christian doctrine in all ages than any other man, was born in Tagasta, a town of Numidia in Africa, in the year 355. His father, Patricius, was a man of good family, though poor; and he was fortunate in having an admirable mother, named Monica, whose tender and Christian care was made, under God, the greatest blessing to her son.

Augustine did not show at first much inclination for study, but he soon got interested in acquiring the art of rhetoric, in which his father anxiously desired that he should excel, intending him to be a pleader of causes in the courts of law. He has himself, in his "Book of Confessions," which is a wonderful record of all his sins and struggles, told us that he fell into many vices when young; and in the midst of the corrupt society into which he was thrown at Carthage, where he was prosecuting his studies, this is not to be wondered at. But at the same time that he fell into vicious ways of living, he became more eagerly bent on the cultivation of his mind, and his progress was very remarkable in all the subjects which he studied. He soon began to be a teacher of rhetoric, but finding that at Carthage the youths who came to his lessons were unruly and ill-conducted, he formed the plan of going to Rome, where he thought he would have a better opportunity for advancement. His father was now dead, and his mother was very averse to his leaving her, so he departed secretly, leaving Monica in bitter grief for his loss. This good mother not only lamented her son's desertion of her, but she grieved also for the irregularities of his life, and for the wild and profane notions on religious subjects which he had adopted. He had become a Manichean, one of the worst sorts of ancient heresy, and which was indeed more like heathenism than Christianity. Monica ceased not to pray night and day for the deliverance of her son from these dangerous errors, and it was not long before her prayers were mercifully answered.

Augustine was not altogether contented with

his success as a teacher at Rome, and the governor of the city having at that time occasion to send an instructor in rhetoric to Milan, he gladly accepted the appointment, which was offered to him, and went to take up his abode in the great city of the north of Italy. Milan was at that time under the pastoral care of the famous Ambrose, who had been advanced to the highest dignity of the Church from a lay office, as has been related in his life. Augustine naturally went to hear a preacher whose fame for eloquence was so great, though he was still strongly opposed to the doctrines which Ambrose so well advocated. The effect of the sermon which he heard from him, was to make him doubtful as to the truth of his Manichean views, though as yet he was not fully convinced of the truth of the orthodox doctrine.

Meantime Monica, his loving mother, unable to endure a longer absence from her son, had followed him from Africa, and now arrived at Milan, while Augustine was still wavering in his convictions on Christian truth. She was delighted to find him in somewhat a more hopeful state than when he had left her, and she redoubled her prayers to Heaven to grant her the blessing of seeing his complete conversion. It would appear that this wished for event came to Augustine in such a way as to show most clearly that it was directly from God and not due to human agency. A bright light seemed gradually to enter his soul. His difficulties began to disappear. He now regarded the Holy Scriptures in a way different from before, and took especial pleasure in studying the Epistles of St. Paul.

Determined now to become a member of the Church, he applied to Ambrose for counsel and guidance, and the good bishop, who was so much occupied with various calls on his time as to be unable to devote much attention to him, after some words of encouragement, sent him to Simplician for further guidance. Simplician was the presbyter who had instructed Ambrose himself in religious knowledge, and no one could have been better fitted to help Augustine in feeling his way to the truth. The path seemed now clear before him as to rejecting the Manichean errors and embracing the true doctrine, but still Augustine shrank from baptism, as not feeling himself strong enough to renounce the pleasures of the world and to adopt a strict religious life. His struggles and inward conflicts were very great, and we may imagine with what interest his mother Monica watched his progress in the reception of Divine grace.

One day Augustine had retired into a garden to meditate and deliberate with himself, when he seemed to hear a number of children's voices constantly repeating the same words—"Take and read," "Take and read." After a time he was led to think that these words had a special reference to himself, and taking in his hand the Epistles of St. Paul, he turned to the first place which presented itself, which was this:—"Not in rioting and drunkenness, nor in chambering and wantonness, not in strife and envying; but put ye on the Lord Jesus Christ, and make not provision for the flesh to fulfil the lusts thereof."* These words made such an impression on Augustine, that he determined no longer to delay a complete devotion to the service of Christ, and his mother Monica's heart was beyond measure rejoiced to hear that he was now desirous of baptism and fully persuaded in his own mind. In order to prepare himself for receiving this great Christian sacrament, Augustine gave up his employment as a teacher of rhetoric, and

* Romans xiii. 13.

ST. AUGUSTINE AND MONICO.—*Page* 267

retired into the country, where he employed himself in prayers and scriptural exercises.

At Easter, in the year 386, he being then thirty-one years old, Augustine was baptized by Ambrose at Milan, and soon afterwards was confirmed and admitted to the Lord's Supper. He welcomed these Christian privileges with the most intense devotion and thankfulness to God, and Monica was allowed to see her son not only reclaimed from an immoral life and from vain opinions, but also showing evidently the work of Christian grace in the soul in its most complete and striking effects.

Augustine now had fully determined altogether to renounce secular pursuits, and to devote himself to the sacred ministry of the Church. In company with a friend named Euodius, who like himself had been baptized and was contemplating taking holy orders, and with his mother Monica, he left Milan, intending to return to his native Africa. But on the journey, when they were at Ostia, near Rome, Monica fell sick, and it was soon seen that her end was approaching. The son and the mother took sweet counsel together, and spoke of the joy of knowing God, and being admitted to a nearer approach to Him as infinitely beyond all earthly things. "My son," said the dying Monica, "this life has now no charms for me. I have nothing now to do here, and nothing to hope for. One thing there was for which I desired to live, namely, that I might see you a true Christian before I died. This God has given me, even beyond my hopes; and now that I perceive you, despising earthly happiness, to have become His true servant, what have I to do here?" Soon afterwards this good woman breathed her last, and in spite of his Christian fortitude, Augustine grieved bitterly at the loss of one so loving and so wise.

After the last offices had been religiously paid to his mother, St. Augustine went to Rome, and feeling that the duty now most incumbent on him was to endeavour to overthrow those mischievous errors of the Manicheans which he had done so much to uphold for many years, he employed himself in writing books against these heretics, in which his great talents and wonderful eloquence are very conspicuous. After remaining some time at Rome, he returned to Africa, and visited his native place, Tagasta, where he sold the little property belonging to the family, and distributed the proceeds among the poor. He now determined to go into complete solitude for some time, that he might have leisure to make himself thoroughly acquainted with the Holy Scriptures. The love which he felt for the Scriptures has probably never been surpassed. " In these," said he, "a man may study himself, as in a mirror, and see what he is and whither he is going. Constant reading of the Scriptures is the great purifier; it puts before the soul the fear of hell, and quickens the heart to seek for heavenly joys. He who would be well with God, ought frequently to read and to pray. When we pray we speak to God, but when we read, God speaks to us. The reading of Holy Scripture gives a twofold gift: it instructs the understanding, and it draws away the reader from the vanities of the world, and leads him to the love of God. Just as by bodily food the body is nourished, so by Divine words the inner man is nourished and fed; as saith the Psalmist—' How sweet are thy words unto my lips, yea sweeter than honey and the honey-comb.' But that man is of all the most blessed who turns the Divine Scriptures into works." *

The fame of Augustine arising from his books

* Sermon 112.

against the Manicheans was now spread throughout Christian Africa, and when, after three years spent in retirement, he had occasion to visit Hippo, an important town on the north coast, afterwards called Bona, the Christians at that place determined to procure his ordination to the priesthood. Although he had long intended to devote himself to the service of the Church, yet Augustine shrank from the great responsibility of the priestly office, out of a deep sense of humility. But, as was often done in those days, a sort of friendly violence was used to him to make him yield, and Valerius, the Bishop of Hippo, ordained him priest. Augustine however refused to enter at once upon the duties of this office. He desired more time for retirement and preparation. When at length he began to appear as a preacher, his power and eloquence at once made a deep impression on all who heard him. Many of those who had been tainted by the Manichean or other errors he now brought back into the right path. But while he preached earnestly to the people at Hippo, he did not neglect a more general care for the Church of God. He continued to write books which might reach Christians more remote from him, and his wonderful industry and rapidity in this work have perhaps never been surpassed.

His fame was now so great, that when a Council of the African Church was held at Hippo, in the year 393, Augustine, though only a presbyter, was appointed to deliver a discourse upon the Creed before the assembled bishops. Many of his brethren now suggested to Valerius, the Bishop of Hippo, how important it was for the interest of the Church that Augustine should be promoted to the highest office in the ministry, and Valerius, eagerly desirous to have him as his coadjutor and successor, applied to the Bishop of Carthage, as primate of the province, for his sanction to this arrangement. This was readily granted, and Augustine was consecrated bishop in the forty-first year of his age, and undertook the charge of the Church of Hippo. His zeal in the performance of his work was very great. It was with difficulty that he was induced to go beyond the limits of his diocese. He used to say that it ought to be a weighty cause which could justify the shepherd in leaving his sheep. When his friends pressed him to come to Carthage, the capital city of the province, and the seat of the Court, he replied that he had no time for such things, that he did not take the episcopal office that he might neglect the care of those who were put under him; on the contrary, he feared that whatever diligence he could use, he should nevertheless at the last day be convicted of negligence. Carthage, he said, could not give him salvation, nor could the Proconsul's court excuse in the sight of God that bishop who had been negligent in the care of his Church.

Yet though he would not leave his diocese for relaxation, or his own pleasure, yet when he considered that the weighty interests of the Church required it, he was ready to do so. On this ground he went on an embassy to Honorius, the Emperor in Italy, to invoke the aid of the State against the Donatists. These were a sect of heretics in North Africa who dissented from the Church more on questions of discipline than doctrine. Their views were unreasonably strict; they would not allow any place of repentance for those who had shown any weakness in the time of persecution, and they held that all who were not living strictly Christian lives, should be at once cut off from the Church. But though they thus contradicted the teaching of our Lord in the parables of the tares and the net, this was not the chief reason which induced Augustine and others to seek to bring the temporal power against them. They were themselves the aggressive party, and were in the habit of assaulting the orthodox Christians with the greatest violence, so that it was only just that the bishops should seek the protection of the civil power against them. Unfortunately, however, they did more than this. Not only did Augustine demand of the Emperor efficient protection and equal laws, but he induced him to decree most severe and persecuting edicts against the Donatists, and he eagerly put these in force in his zeal for the Church, and under the belief that by so doing he could restore unity. But not only did persecution in his case, as in all others, fail to produce the effects at which it aimed, but it had the result of making the Donatist faction so hostile and vindictive, that afterwards, when the Vandals invaded Africa, they gave a ready and eager support to them, and thus helped to overthrow the Roman power in that province.

After the persecution of the Donatists had endured some time, a great Council was held at Carthage, in which Augustine presided, and the errors of the Donatists having been condemned, many of them, wearied of the strife, consented to submit to the Church, while others, more obstinate, only prepared for more vigorous resistance.

Augustine was now called upon to contend against a set of heretics of very different opinions. Pelagius, whose real name is thought to have been Morgan, a monk born in Britain, had begun to teach, both in lectures and in writings, that the views held by the Church on original sin, on grace and free will, were not in accordance with Scripture and reason. He held that the fall of Adam, although it brought sin into the world, and with it misery and death, yet had not necessarily polluted and corrupted the nature of man to such an extent, that every one born into the world inherited a sinful nature. He held also that a man by his own will, and aided by grace, could reach absolute perfection in this life.* These views, though they did not contradict any article of the Creed, were in many ways mischievous and dangerous, and Augustine spent a great part of his life in combating them, and composed many of his most powerful treatises with that object. In doing so he was gradually led to change the views about free will and grace

* See the Life of St. Jerome.

which he had originally held, and to attribute almost entirely the work of conversion and sanctification to the irresistible grace of God, on which point he has gone further than any of the other Fathers, and is thought by many to have left no place for the free will of man. In reading these and others of Augustine's writings, we are struck by his wonderful power of applying Scripture, as well as by the devotional spirit which always animates him, and by the eloquence which breathes in all his words. No man perhaps ever wrote more earnestly and more convincingly—his words always seem to come from the heart.

Augustine was at this time the moving spirit of the Christian world, all difficult questions were brought to him, all who needed counsel and help flocked to him, and yet with all this he ceased not to pour forth abundant store of learned writings, so that the work which he accomplished was indeed prodigious. In order to get through it, he made a most exact arrangement of his time, and he was wont to say, that he took example by men of business, who were so exact and regular in all their money transactions and who put off refreshment and repose until all was accurately settled.

He never refused to see any that came to him. He was ever ready to throw himself eagerly into their difficulties, and he strove, like the Roman Emperor, never to let a petitioner go away from him in sadness. The door of his room ever stood open, and all might resort to him who pleased; but so great was his power of abstraction, that it often happened that he was perfectly unconscious of the presence of a visitor, even when he was addressed and his help invoked. He was very zealous in trying to settle all disputes between members of his flock, and to make them dwell in brotherly love and charity; but this occupied a great deal of his time, so quarrelsome and contentious were his people. The one thing which he neglected in connexion with his bishopric was to look carefully after the administration of its revenues. Careless as he was about wealth and only desirous for increase of spiritual treasures, he left these matters to others and gave himself entirely up to occupations of a more spiritual character.

We cannot here give any full account of the numerous valuable treatises which Augustine wrote. There was not an heretical nor false opinion of his day which he did not combat in writing, and scarcely a part of Scripture which he has not illustrated by his Commentaries, Homilies, and Sermons. Two writings he composed which have a special interest in connexion with his own character. The one was his "Confessions," which has been already referred to, and which is a most wonderful setting forth of the feelings of a soul deeply impressed with a sense of sin, and a burning love and devotion to the Saviour of sinners. The other was the "Book of Retractations," which is perhaps even more wonderful than the "Confessions," inasmuch as people are often more ready to acknowledge themselves to have been wrong morally than to have been mistaken in their opinions and statements. But this is what Augustine does at great length in his "Retractations," and this book has been very well described as "one of the noblest sacrifices ever laid on the altar of truth by a majestic intellect acting in obedience to the purest conscientiousness."[*]

There is also another work of Augustine's which we must mention, which may, perhaps, be considered the greatest work composed by him, or any of the Fathers. This is his famous treatise on the "City of God," a very long and learned

[*] Smith's "Biographical Dictionary:" Art. Augustine.

work, the object of which we will let him describe in his own words:—" In the meantime Rome was overthrown by the irruption of the Goths under King Alaric and the mighty slaughter which followed. Upon this the worshippers of false gods, whom we call Pagans, tried to throw the blame of this upon the Christian religion, and more fiercely even than their wont, began to blaspheme the true God. Inflamed by zeal for the House of God, I determined to write the book on the 'City of God' against their blasphemies and errors. This work occupied me a good many years, as I was often interrupted by other matters. At length the great treatise on the 'City of God' was finished in twenty-two books. The five first books are meant to refute those who think they cannot have prosperity without the worship of many gods. The next five are directed against those who, though they don't expect prosperity to come to them by this worship, yet think their worship right on religious grounds. Then, that we may not only refute others, but also set forth our own doctrines, the second part of the work, contained in twelve books, is given up to this. The four first contain the origin of those two cities or states of which one is of God, the other of this world. The second four relate the growth of these, and the last four their destined terminations. The twenty-two books are composed on both the cities or states, but they take their name only from the more excellent, namely, 'the City of God."'*

This great work then may be considered as the last important work written by Christian writers against the heathen superstitions of the old Greeks and Romans. It completed the downfall of the Pagan faith, and henceforth we don't hear much of it. It gradually languished and died away.

The great learning and eloquence of Augustine, as well as his earnest piety and devotion, became famous throughout the whole Christian world. The Church rejoiced in him as in a most complete champion, armed at all points to contend for the truth. The labours which he performed in writing, preaching, and deciding causes seem almost more than it was possible for one man to have supported, yet for many years he continued to carry them on. As age, however, grew upon him, and his strength diminished, he determined to take an assistant in his work as a bishop, and appointed one of his presbyters, named Eradius,

* Augustine, "Retractations," b. ii.

to this office, with an understanding that he should succeed him in the see at his death. He now devoted himself entirely to those learned writings which were of such great value to the Church at large. But these quiet employments which he had marked out for the evening of his days were soon rudely interfered with by the troubles which broke out in North Africa.

A man of great influence under the Roman Emperor, Count Boniface, believing himself unjustly treated by the Emperor, had fled into Spain, and had there stirred up the barbarian Vandals, who had occupied that country, to invade the Roman province of Africa. They gladly consented to his proposals, and entering Africa with large forces, spread destruction and ruin everywhere, and in particular drove out the orthodox priests and bishops from their churches, setting in their places those who professed the Arian heresy, which was the religion of the Vandals. Boniface was soon seized with compunction for what he had done in bringing ruin on his country, and having obtained the Emperor's pardon, was now eagerly ready to make war upon the Vandals, and, if possible, to drive them out of the country. His troops were, however, defeated, and he was driven with them and a large number of fugitives from all parts of the province to shut himself up in Hippo, the city in which Augustine lived. The Vandals soon came to besiege this place, and now, Augustine, seeing how important it was that the courage and spirits of the people should be kept up, employed himself in earnestly exhorting all to be of good heart, to try to please God by devoting themselves to His service, and to have faith in His providential care. The place was crowded with those who needed care both as to their bodies and their souls, and the great exertions which Augustine was obliged to make proved too much for his frame, weakened by age and labour, and he was soon stretched on a bed of sickness, with but small prospect of his recovery. As he saw his end approaching, he displayed the greatest devotion. He desired that he might now be left alone, except for the attendance necessary for his sickness, and he gave his whole time to prayer and contemplation. He was wont to say that no one ought to desire to quit this world without a suitable amount of bodily pain, to wean his cares and affections away from the world. Over his bed he had hung up the seven penitential psalms, which he frequently repeated with

great fervour. One of his last prayers was—
" Grant to me, O God, the pardon of my sins, and
that presently when I have laid aside the burden
of the flesh, I may enter into thy joys, O heavenly
Jerusalem, and may have true rest there. Grant
that I may enter within the walls of Thy beau-
teous city, and may receive a crown from the
hand of my Lord. May I be allowed to join
those most holy bands, and with the blessed spirits
assist in glorifying the Creator, and enjoying the
supreme happiness which is theirs." As long as
he could speak he continued to exhort those near
him to holiness of life, and to call upon his
Saviour; and at length his bodily powers completely failed, and he fell asleep in Jesus, in the
year of our Lord 430, in the seventy-sixth year
of his age, and the thirty-sixth of his episcopate.
He was mercifully taken away from the evil
which was to come, for soon after his death
Hippo was captured by the Vandals, and every
sort of cruelty and outrage was perpetrated by
them, especially against the clergy.

GREGORY THE GREAT.

Gregory, surnamed the Great, and frequently described as the fourth great doctor of the Latin Church, was born in Rome, about the year 540. He was of noble descent, and his family united both the civil and ecclesiastical dignity. His father Gordian was a senator; a Pope (Felix II.) was among his ancestors; two sainted virgins, Thersilla and Silvia, were his aunts. To his noble descent was added considerable wealth, all of which, as soon as he became master of it, was directed to religious uses. He founded and endowed, probably from estates in Sicily, six monasteries in that island, and a seventh in Rome, which he chose for his own retreat; the remainder of his goods he distributed among the poor, and "he who was wont to go in grand state through the city covered with silks and jewels, was content to be clad in a mean garment, and himself a poor man, to minister to the poor." Entering his Roman monastery as a simple monk, he distinguished himself by his devotional exercises and excessive asceticism, although his health was very infirm, and he was subject to frequent and alarming fainting fits.

It may have been that Gregory's devotion would have been as great had he lived at any other period, but the character of the time in which he lived had a special effect upon his mind, inasmuch as he was convinced by the troubles and iniquities which then abounded, that the day of judgment was close at hand. At this time the Lombards, a fierce nation of northern origin, were invading and desolating Italy. These savage warriors had no awe for religion; they burned churches, laid waste monasteries, slew ecclesiastics, and ill-treated consecrated virgins. In their wars carried on in Italy with the troops of the Greek Emperor, the most dreadful cruelties were perpetrated, until at length Italy and the persecuted Church were relieved from their hated presence by the succour afforded by the Franks.

In the various Lives of Gregory which have been compiled by early writers, a vast amount of miraculous occurrences are said to have taken place at the monastery of St. Andrew, where he dwelt. These stories show the great veneration which attached to his name and character, but it cannot be said that all of them exhibit him in a very pleasing light. For instance, it is said that when Gregory was abbot, an unfortunate monk, who had tenderly nursed him when ill, was lying at the point of death, and in that condition disclosed to the abbot, who was sitting near him, the fact that he had three pieces of gold secreted among his possessions. This was against the rules of the order, and Gregory, excited to wrath, took vengeance upon the dying man, by allowing no one to approach him, or to minister to him, and on his death having his body cast out upon the dunghill with his gold; all the monks at the same time shouting, "Thy money perish with thee." This conduct, as has been well observed, exhibits "ingratitude and cruelty under the guise of duty." *

It was while he was abbot at St. Andrew's that the event happened by which Gregory is perhaps best known to us now, and which had such an important influence on the future of England. We will give this in the words in which it is related by John the Deacon:—"On a

* Milman.

certain day, it chanced that a large number of traders had lately arrived, and a great quantity of merchandise was exhibited for sale in the Roman market, together with a numerous assemblage of purchasers. It chanced then that Gregory, that most worthy man of God, passed by, and that he seeing among other things some boys of fair skin and of most remarkable beauty, especially distinguished by the brightness of their hair, offered for sale, asked the merchant from what country he had brought them. He answered, 'They come from the island of Britain, all the inhabitants of which have a similar fair and bright appearance.' Gregory then said, 'Are these islanders Christians, or are they in the bondage of heathen error?' The merchant answered, 'They are not Christians, but are held fast in the meshes of heathenism.' Then Gregory, groaning deeply, said, 'Alas! that the Prince of Darkness should have as his own these bright faces, and that so great beauty of looks should be joined to a mind empty of the grace of God.' Again he asked what was the name of that race. 'They are called Angles.' Then he—'It is well! Angles, as it were angels, for they have angelic looks, and such as these ought to be fellow-citizens with the angels in heaven.' Again he asked what the province was called. The merchant answered, 'The men of that province are called Deiri.' Then Gregory: 'This too is well that they should be called Deiri, for they must be rescued from wrath (*de irâ*) and called to the grace of Christ. How is the king of that province named?' The merchant answered, ' He is named Ælla.' Then Gregory, playing on the name, said, 'It is well that the king is called Ælla, for it is fitting that Alleluia in praise of the Creator should be chanted in those regions.' Then going presently to Benedict, pontiff of the Apostolical See, he began to urge vehemently that he should send some ministers of the Word into Britain. But as the Pope did not know of any one who was willing to go, Gregory did not hesitate to urge himself for the office, until the Pope granted him leave. And with the greatest reluctance of the whole clergy and people he allowed Gregory in his eager desire to set out, praying for the Divine blessing on his ministrations."

Gregory had travelled three days' journey on his charitable mission, when he was overtaken by messengers sent to recall him. Rome had risen in mutiny, and compelled the Pope to revoke his decision. We shall see later on, how Gregory's good intentions towards Britain, of which he never lost sight, were ultimately carried out. Gregory was now no longer allowed to remain in the quiet of his monastery, but was brought out to be employed in the public affairs of the Church. He was sent as the representative of the Pope to Constantinople, to endeavour to obtain the aid of the Greek Emperor against the Lombards. Here in the midst of secular affairs he still lived a life of strict religious observance, and it was now that he began and wrote a considerable portion of his treatise on the Book of Job (called "Magna Moralia"), which is perhaps the greatest of his works. This treatise is one of the most striking examples to be found in the writings of the Fathers of mystical meanings assigned to the words of Scripture. Gregory sees the germs of all Christian doctrines in the ancient poetical language of this grand book, but that he was not calculated to throw much light upon the interpretation of Job, we may infer from the fact that he was quite ignorant of Oriental languages, customs, and manners, and that he did not even understand Greek.[*]

[*] As he himself tells us in his Epistle.

Great calamities now pressed upon the city of Rome. The Lombards threatened it, and the Greek Emperor could furnish no aid. The Tiber overflowed its banks, and swept away the granaries of corn. A dreadful pestilence followed, of which Pope Pelagius was one of the first victims. All eyes were at once turned towards Gregory as the successor of Pelagius, but Gregory himself dreaded the high post, and used every means that he could devise to escape it. He willingly, however, took the direction of affairs in endeavouring to work upon the people to show a general and deep penitence for their sins, if perhaps the wrath of God might be averted. Having addressed to them a sermon of great earnestness, he arranged solemn processions, seven in number, to include the whole city, which were to make the round of the churches, and to put up humble prayers for the deliverance of the city from the pestilence. During the time that these litanies were proceeding, no less than eighty persons fell dead from the pestilence, but Gregory persevered in his exhortations, and soon an abatement of the scourge was experienced.

There is no reason to suppose that Gregory was anything but sincere in his wish to avoid the popedom. Generally this reluctance has only been a mere empty farce, but it was not so with Gregory. He loved the quiet, contemplative life of the cloister, and he understood better than any man of his day the vast labours entailed upon him who, in those troublous days, should be Patriarch of the West, if the office was to be performed as such a man as Gregory would feel bound to perform it. At once, on his being compelled to take on him this responsible post, Gregory's life became altogether different from what it had previously been. He plunged into business with most intense earnestness. Nothing was too great, nothing too little for his attention. It is impossible to contemplate without admiration such a life of vigorous usefulness, such a dedication of the highest faculties to the service of Christ.

While Gregory knew well the dignity of the place to which he had been called, he yet shrank from those proud assumptions into which his successors unfortunately fell. Nothing seemed to him more blasphemous and intolerable than the title of "*universal bishop*," which the Patriarch of Constantinople had lately assumed, and he was the first Pope to use the style, which in him was not a mere pretence, of " servant of the servants of God." Writing to expostulate with the Emperor Maurice against Archbishop John's use of the proud title of "universal bishop," Gregory says, "Let all Christian hearts reject the *blasphemous* name. It was once applied by the Council of Chalcedon in honour of St. Peter to the Bishop of Rome, but the more humble pontiffs of Rome would not assume a title injurious to the rest of the priesthood. I am but the servant of those priests who live according to their order."*

The energetic bishop at once set himself to reform all the abuses which he found prevailing in the Church. Among these, one was the ill manner in which the service of the Church was sung, the want of order in the directions, and the badness of the music. To remedy this, Gregory made some changes in the services for the administration of the sacraments, and compiled a volume containing them, called a *Sacramentary*. As parts of the service were to be chanted, these were put into another volume, called an *Antiphonary*, because all the chanting was alternate between two divisions and sides of the choir. The Lessons were written in a *Lectionary*, the

* Gregory, Epist. ad Maurit. iv.

Psalms in a *Psalter*, and the general directions or Rubrics in a book called *The Order*.* To improve the music of the chanting, Gregory took great pains. He introduced a new mode of chanting, which still bears his name, and which was an improvement on the old mode established by St. Ambrose; he formed musical schools for learning his method, and himself gave lessons in it; and when John the Deacon wrote his Life (ninth century), there were still to be seen at the Lateran palace the couch on which he reclined while teaching, the whip with which he used to punish the carelessness of the boys, and the original copy of his *Antiphonary*, with the portions marked for each day.

Another point to which Gregory paid great attention was the management and distribution of the revenues of his see. He made careful regulations for protecting the poor peasants, as also the rights and interests of the farmer, and while everything was done consistent with justice and equity to increase the revenues of the Church, those revenues when received were distributed to the people with unexampled liberality. The sick and infirm were superintended by persons appointed to inspect every street. Before the Pope

* Fleury, xxxvi. 15.

sat down to his own meal, a portion was separated and sent out to the hungry at his door. A beggar chancing one day to die of want without obtaining relief, Gregory condemned himself to a hard penance for the guilt of this neglect.

While thus active at Rome, Gregory also exercised a watchful superintendence over all the bishops of the West, and removed and deposed many of them for various crimes. But his most noble work was his earnest solicitude in spreading the Gospel. In Spain, and in Christian Africa, he effected much in extending and strengthening the orthodox religion, and we in England have great cause to revere his missionary zeal and activity. We have seen how he had, before succeeding to the popedom, been captivated by the Anglo-Saxon slaves, and he did not forget their country when he had greater power to help them. In the fourth year of his pontificate he selected from the monastery of St. Andrew a monk named Augustine, with some other monks, and dispatched them to Britain, to endeavour to find a footing in that country for the spreading of the Gospel among the Saxons. The monks, accustomed to the quiet life of the cloister, lost heart after a few days' travel, and sent Augustine back to the

Pope to represent the dangers and difficulties of the undertaking, their ignorance of the language, and their wish to be relieved from the task imposed upon them. Upon this, Gregory sent Augustine back again to them with a letter as follows:—" Gregory, bishop, servant of the servants of God, to the servants of our Lord Jesus Christ. It were better not to begin a good thing, than when it is begun to turn back from it upon consideration; wherefore it behoves you, beloved brethren, to fulfil with the greatest zeal, God helping you, the good work which you have begun. Let not the labour of the journey nor the tongues of evil-speaking men frighten you; but with all earnestness and zeal perform what, at God's prompting, ye have begun, knowing that though the labour be great, the greater will be the glory of the eternal reward which ye shall obtain. When Augustine, your leader, whom we have appointed your abbot, returns to you, in all things obey him humbly, knowing that whatever you shall perform at his admonition will be profitable to your souls. May God Almighty protect you with His grace, and grant me to see in the eternal fatherland the fruit of your labour, inasmuch as, though I am unable to work with you, I would be found with you in the joy of your reward, because truly I desire to labour with you." Augustine was further directed to obtain episcopal consecration from Etherius, Bishop of Arles, and Gregory wrote to the King and Queen of the Franks to assist him in his mission.

Thus encouraged, the monks went on their way, and the result of their labours was soon seen in the rapid spread of Christianity among the heathen Saxons. In the directions which Gregory gave them for their work, much wisdom and prudence are displayed. He advised them not to seek for the destruction of the pagan temples, but that they should sanctify them for the performance of Christian worship, the idols only being destroyed. The great feasts which the Saxons had been wont to make to their idols he advised should be still kept up, only on Christian holidays, and in a Christian fashion; and when Augustine sent to enquire whether in religious services he was to observe strictly the use of the Roman Church or to adopt that of Gaul, which differed somewhat from it, Gregory gave him full liberty to select from any Church whatever he thought most conducive to edification. "For" he wrote, "things are not to be preferred on account of the places in which they are found, but when the things are good, then they recommend their place. Choose, then, from all the Churches those things which are pious, right, and religious, and collecting these as it were in a vessel, pour them forth on the table of the Angles, to be their custom."

The wisdom and moderation displayed in these directions contributed doubtless in no small degree to the success of the mission of Augustine. Gratifying accounts were sent to the Pope of the progress of the work, and at the same time he was asked to send them some assistants. This was at once complied with: Mellitus, Justus, Paulinus, Ruffinianus, and others were sent with church-plate, vestments, books, to help forward the mission-work. All of these were active instruments in the conversion of the Saxons, especially Paulinus, who was the first converter of Northumbria and Mercia. The good Pope thus saw the fruit of his labours.

In another way also did Gregory labour for the conversion of the Saxons. He endeavoured to discover any young children of the race who had been sold into slavery, and redeeming them from their masters, to have them instructed in Christianity. His zeal to propagate the Gospel by all legitimate means was unbounded, but he utterly refused to lend his sanction to some of the violent and persecuting measures used in his day. Thus he condemned the forcible baptism of Jews, which had been resorted to in Gaul, declaring that kindness and persuasion were the only legitimate weapons to use for producing conviction. He would not allow the Jews to be forcibly driven out of a country where they had settled, nor would he permit the bishops to seize upon their synagogues to be used as chapels.

While he thus cared for the heathen and protected the Jews, Gregory's watchful discipline endeavoured to enforce earnest diligence and purity among the chief pastors of the Church. He stedfastly opposed pluralities, saying that it was not possible for one who held two offices or cures to give the fitting attention to each. Corrupt and simoniacal promotions in the Church found in him a terrible foe, one who was both able and willing to strike.

Eminent as Gregory was above all bishops of his time, and wielding as he did his authority for the most noble ends, he yet, as we have seen, shrank with indignation from those blasphemous assumptions which his successors at Rome have since made. "No one in the Church," he writes to Archbishop John, "has yet dared to usurp the name of universal bishop. Whoever calls himself universal bishop is Antichrist."*

In the person of Gregory, the Bishop of Rome first became a temporal sovereign. A certain amount of temporal power was forced upon him by the necessities of his situation. The barbarous and savage Lombards were threatening the city; the Eastern Emperor was powerless to help; it became the incumbent duty of the chief man in the city to put himself forward as a leader for the purposes of self-defence; and this Gregory did, and his authority was recognised and obeyed in Rome and Italy, although the Greek Emperor did not admit it. When the Lombard army appeared before the gates of Rome, Gregory was occupied in preaching to the people. He suddenly brought to an end his Commentary on the Temple of Ezekiel, and prepared for a different labour. His Commentary ends with these words—"If I must now break off my discourse, ye are my witnesses for what reason, ye who share in my tribulations. On all sides we are girt with war, everywhere is the imminent peril of death. Some return to us

* Letter to John, Archbishop, Greg. Epist. iv. 38.

with their hands chopped off, some are reported as captives, others as slain. I am constrained to cease from my exposition, for I am weary of life. Who can expect me now to devote myself to sacred eloquence, now that my harp is turned to mourning, and my speech to the voice of them that weep?"

By his energy the city was saved. At the same time Gregory was striving in another and more congenial way to obtain a triumph over the fierce Lombards. The religion which they professed was the Arian form of Christianity, which made them bitterly hostile to all who held Trinitarian orthodoxy. But their king had married a princess named Theodelinda, who had been brought up in the orthodox faith, and Gregory appealed to her to try to stop the ferocious attacks of the Lombards upon the Church, and by her influence with the king he succeeded in doing so. Gradually the true faith spread itself among these barbarous people, and before Gregory's death he had the satisfaction of seeing the good work accomplished. It is said that their king Agilulf restored the wealth which he had plundered from the Churches, reinstated the exiled bishops, and gave great sums for religious purposes.

The Emperor Maurice seems to have persistently refused to assist Gregory or to recognise his services against the Lombards; but that did not excuse the Roman bishop for rejoicing at his barbarous murder by the usurper Phocas, and for calling heaven and earth to exult at the dreadful barbarities which were perpetrated upon him and his family.

Absorbed by his zeal for the advancement of the Church, Gregory, like other good men of similarly impetuous character, did not enough consider the ways and means which were to work the end which he had in view. Confident in his divine mission, and eager to advance the cause of religion by every method, it can hardly be doubted that he lent himself to sanction and even to originate many untrue and ridiculous stories of pretended miracles. In the dialogues which he composed for Queen Theodelinda, are to be found stories so wild and foolish that it is hardly possible to believe that a man like Gregory could have himself credited what he put forth as undoubted facts.

In his practical life as a bishop and administrator of the power belonging to his see, Gregory stands in the very foremost rank, but the puerile superstition which disfigures his writings separates him by a long interval from Augustine, Jerome, and Ambrose and the great Fathers of the fourth century.

In the history of the dark ages of the Church after the time of Gregory, nothing is so offensive as the constant repetition of absurd stories of pretended miracles, wrought by what were called the relics of the saints. The relics supposed to have this wondrous power were eagerly sought after, and often purchased at very high prices. No church or monastery considered itself sufficiently endowed without possessing some of them, and every sort of deceit and lying is connected with their acquisition. For all this the great name of Gregory, who lent himself in an especial manner to magnifying the importance of these relics, is specially responsible. In some points therefore Gregory was by no means in advance of his age, while in other ways he seems to stand out as almost the only great figure between the times of Jerome and Augustine and those of St. Bernard.

Perhaps what we admire most in Gregory is his strict and impartial justice. In his time and according to his own view the life of the cloister was held to be so far more meritorious and excellent than the ordinary life, that when a man had betaken himself to it, not even the most sacred obligations were to be held sufficient to make it fitting for him to abandon it. Gregory, however, would not allow a priest who had taken the vows without the consent of his wife to remain a monk, but obliged him to return to his wife.* When persons had taken sanctuary in a church on account of danger threatened to them, he would not allow the sanctuary to be extended to them unless they were willing to undergo a fair trial, that it might be ascertained whether they were worthy of the protection or not.†

It has been already said that Gregory was constantly impressed with the idea that the end of the world was at hand. The terrible troubles with which all Europe was being afflicted in his day from the wars carried on by the barbarous nations which had invaded the old Roman empire, convinced him that the signs of the latter days were present. From that troublous scene in which he was forced to play a part, and in which his great qualities made him play an earnest and important part, Gregory desired above all things

* Greg. Epist. xi. 50.   † Epist. x. 38.

to be removed, thinking that to be with Christ was indeed far better. In the thirteenth year of his pontificate, A.D. 604, his desire was granted, and this great and energetic Pope, the greatest probably who ever filled the pontifical throne, departed to his rest.

THE VENERABLE BEDE.

In the Life of Gregory the Great, it has been related how that good Pope, full of missionary zeal, dispatched Augustine and his companions to the shores of Britain to convert the Saxons. There can be no clearer proof of the astonishing success of the work of these Christian teachers than the life of him who has been ever distinguished in Church history as the Venerable Bede. Not much more than seventy years after the landing of the Roman missionaries on the savage, turbulent, and heathen island, a native Saxon is found devoting a long and peaceful life to religious and literary study, composing large volumes of theology, explanations of the Scriptures, Church history and poetry, and taking a leading place in the estimation of his contemporaries as one of the chief, if not the chief, religious writer of his day.

The life and work of Bede are indeed wonderful, and all that we know of him gives us a very high idea of his pure and simple Christian character. Unfortunately, however, the amount of our knowledge is but small as far as regards any actions of Bede's life. His life was passed in his monastery in a continual course of study. He took no part in the ecclesiastical controversies and quarrels of the time. Owing, as he did, much to the Roman missionaries and their work, and much also to the Christian teaching which had come from Scotland and the disciples of St Columba, he wrote in his History, in a fair and candid spirit, of the whole process by which England became Christian, after having in a great measure lost the faith which existed among the early Britons. His History is the most valuable work which he composed. His Commentaries on the Scriptures were, indeed, highly valuable for the men of his day; but they consist almost entirely of selections from the Christian Fathers, and his poetry is not of a very high order.

Bede was born in the year 673, at a village between the Wear and the Tyne; a year before the foundation of that monastery at Wearmouth, in which, and its sister house at Jarrow, he was destined to pass his life. Everywhere throughout Europe, when Christianity was first established in a land, it was the care of the great and influential in Church and State to found and endow monasteries. And, indeed, we can easily understand the absolute necessity of doing this. It was absolutely necessary that religious-minded persons should be brought into a sacred building, and thus protected from violence; that they should be housed and fed, and thus have time for learning the faith, for religious services, and for preparing themselves to influence others.

In those dark times when there were no books, no roads, no security for property, the flickering light of Christianity could only be kept alive by these great religious houses. It was thus that Aidan, the holy bishop, who had come from St. Columba's Isle of Saints in the north, to preach the Gospel in Northumberland, founded a monastery on Holy Isle; and it was a monk of this house, called Benedict Biscop, who founded the monasteries of Wearmouth and Jarrow, who was the patron of Bede from the age of seven years, and who, by his wisdom and liberality, did a great work in spreading the Gospel among his fellow-countrymen. For not only did Benedict go into Gaul to get masons to build his monasteries, but he also made frequent journeys to Rome to purchase manuscript books, and altogether procured a considerable number for the library at Wearmouth. It was from the books thus procured that Bede himself learned and then became the teacher of others. He was the founder of theological learning in England. " He was the interpreter of the thoughts of ages to a race utterly unacquainted even with the names of the great men of Pagan and Christian antiquity." * When we think of him in this light, his mission and his work must appear to us very striking and important. He was in an especial way one of the *Fathers* of the English Church.

If Augustine, Aidan, and others, some coming from Rome, and some from quarters independent of Rome, were the converters of the Saxons, Bede, himself a Saxon, was their great instructor. The first Saxon converts, being little better than savages, could not be taught much beyond the very elements of the faith. It is said that the whole knowledge of even some of the teachers was contained in the Creed and the Lord's Prayer. Some were entirely ignorant of Latin; for these Bede translated into Anglo-Saxon the most ne-

* Milman.

cessary formularies. He was the great schoolmaster of the Anglo-Saxon race.

Being born on the land belonging to the monastery of Wearmouth, Bede, according to the law then prevailing, was absolutely the property of that establishment. Thus, at seven years of age he was delivered to the Abbot Benedict for instruction, and under him and his successor Ceolfrid he was educated. But the short and simple sketch which he has left us of his own life ought to be inserted without alteration. He thus ends his Ecclesiastical History:—

"This much touching the ecclesiastical history of the Britons, and especially of the English nation, as I could learn by the writings of my ancestors, by the tradition of my elders, or by my own knowledge, I have by the help of God brought unto this order and issue, I, Bede, the servant of God, and priest of the monastery of the blessed Apostles Peter and Paul at Wearmouth. Which being born in the territory of the said monastery, when I was seven years of age I was delivered by the hands of my friends and kinsfolks to be brought up of the most reverend Abbot Benet, and afterwards to Ceolfrid. From the which time, spending all the days of my life in the mansion of the same monastery, I applied all my study to the meditation of Holy Scripture; and observing withal the regular discipline, and keeping the daily singing of God's service in the church, the rest of the time I was delighted always to learn of others, to teach myself, or else to write. In the nineteenth year of my age I was made deacon, and in the thirtieth year priest; both which orders I received by the hands of the most reverend bishop, John of Beverley, at the commandment of Ceolfrid, my abbot. From which time of my priesthood, until the year of my age fifty-nine, I have upon Holy Scripture, for my own instruction and others, partly briefly noted and gathered what other holy Fathers have written, partly I have at large expounded after the manner of their interpretation and meaning."*

This was the life of the Venerable Bede, and this tells us all that there really is to be told about him. The fame of his studies and his devotion could not fail to be spread abroad in the Church, and Sergius, the Roman pontiff, endeavoured to induce Bede to quit his peaceful retreat and to come to Rome; but this he refused to do, not

* Quoted from a translation of the sixteenth century.

being able to abandon the studies which he loved so dearly.

Some few particulars of Bede's last hours have been preserved to us by historians. When about sixty years of age he became subject to asthma. This disorder came on him violently one year about the time of Easter, and rapidly growing worse, Bede perceived that his end was approaching. On Ascension-day he was drawing near to the last struggle, but he was still eagerly bent to finish a translation of St. John's Gospel into the Saxon tongue. From early morning until the afternoon he kept his pupils employed in writing, when all but one youth left him to join in the procession usual on that day. "A single chapter yet remains," the lad remarked. "Dearest master, will it distress you if I ask you to go on with its translation?" The dying scholar answered: "By no means; take your pen, but write quickly." As time thus wore away, the venerable translator said: "There are a few pleasing trifles in my desk—a little pepper, some handkerchiefs, and incense; run, bring them to me, and call my brother-priests; I would fain distribute among these friends such little marks of my kind regard as God has given me. Rich men's presents are

BEDE TRANSLATING ST. JOHN'S GOSPEL.—*Page* 311.

gold and silver, or other costly things; mine must be recommended by the affectionate pleasure which I feel in bestowing them." The young secretary did as he was bid, and Bede's weeping friends were soon collected around him. " You will see my face no more," said Bede, " on this side of another world. It is time that my spirit should return to Him who gave it. My life has been long, and a gracious Providence has made it happy; the time of my dissolution is at hand, I have a desire to depart and to be with Christ." In the midst of this pious and affecting language, the youth suddenly interposed: " Master, one sentence has even yet not been written." He was answered: " Make haste, then, and write it." This done, the sinking teacher said: " It is finished. Take my head and turn my face to the spot where I have been used to pray. Glory to the Father, the Son, and the Holy Ghost." His lips immediately ceased to move, and those who stood around him saw that his pure and holy spirit had passed away.*

Bede was first buried at the monastery where he died, but afterwards his remains were removed

* Soames's " Anglo-Saxon Church."

to Durham, and buried in the same tomb with those of St. Cuthbert.

For some centuries after the death of Bede, the Anglo-Saxon Church was the most enlightened in Europe, and greater knowledge, purer doctrine, and higher morality were to be found in it than anywhere on the Continent. Alcuin and others went out from it to be the instructors of other Churches. But in the ninth, tenth, and eleventh centuries there was a continued increase of darkness, ignorance, and corruption throughout the West. These centuries are usually and rightly called the Dark Ages. The first beginning of improvement was effected by the great man whose life we are now about to relate—St. Bernard, often called "the last of the Fathers."

ST. BERNARD.

St. Bernard was the great religious reformer of the twelfth century, and by his extraordinary personal gifts exercised an authority and influence greater perhaps than any other individual man in a similar position has ever exercised. He changed the whole character of the monastic orders, he reformed the secular clergy, he made and directed popes, he bent all the crowned heads of Europe to his will, he aroused the religious zeal of all the chivalry of the West, and caused it to pour itself forth in vast numbers in the attempt to wrest the Holy Land from the Mussulmans. There was no corner of Europe in which his influence was not felt, and scarce any man of his day who did not look up to him with profound reverence and admiration. It was thought that he could work miracles with the most complete ease, and that he was able to predict the future; that he possessed the knowledge of all truth, and wielded all supernatural power at his will. The life of such a man must be worthy of careful consideration, simply from the effect which he produced on others, even if there were nothing in his own character or writings specially remarkable. But this is far from being the case.

St. Bernard's character was distinguished by intense devotion, and a burning love of that which he thought to be right; he was above selfish ends and petty meanness. His writings exhibit purity and holiness of thought, a hatred of every form of vice, and an ardent love of God. At the same time there was in St. Bernard, as in all human characters, much that fell short of perfection. He was a bigoted zealot of asceticism, by which he injured his own health and much impaired his usefulness; he was fiery and passionate in his temper, which sometimes led him into injustice, and he was not sufficiently scrupulous about the means employed if he held the end to be good.

Bernard was born at Fontaines, near Dijon, in Burgundy, in the year 1091. His father, Tecelin, a knight of an ancient and noble family, was occupied with deeds of arms, and left the care of his sons to his wife Aletta, a woman of great devotion and gentleness of character. Her religion took the form usual in that day of great admiration of the life of the cloister, and she desired to see all her seven children take religious vows. In her own house she imitated as much as possible the state of a convent, and Bernard soon learned to be all that his mother desired in his wish for the monastic life. He was sent to Chatillon to be instructed for the priesthood, but his mother dying soon afterwards, and some of the young nobles of his acquaintance endeavouring to allure him to a worldly life, Bernard hesitated, and was inclined to turn to secular studies. But his mother seemed to appear to him in a dream and chide him, and so he again returned to his former purpose. Full of zeal himself, he endeavoured also to work upon others, and succeeded in persuading his uncle and all his brothers to join him in becoming monks. They lived together practising strict discipline in a house at Chatillon, and in the meantime Bernard was deliberating to what religious house and order he and his friends should attach themselves. To one of such devotion as Bernard possessed the choice was not easy.

At that time great licentiousness and corruption pervaded all classes in Europe, and the monasteries had been completely overwhelmed by the prevailing laxity of manners. Let Bernard himself describe for us the state of the houses specially dedicated to religion.

"How is it that we see such deplorable excess in diet, such luxury in dress, in the coverings of the beds, in the equipages, the horses, the structure of the buildings? The greater the excess the more flourishing is said to be the state of religion. Economy now passes for avarice, sobriety for ill-breeding, and silence for melancholy; and, on the contrary, laxity goes by the name of discretion, and profusion by that of liberality; continual talking is considered a proof of civility, and laughter and mockery of gaiety of heart. Superfluity is called charity, and this false charity saps the foundations of the true. How can that be charity which provides for the flesh and neglects the spirit? or that discretion which gives all to the body and nothing to the soul? Nay, that is neither charity nor discretion, but imprudence, which cherishes the passions and lusts of the flesh, and labours not after the cultivation of the virtues. The Scriptures, the salvation of souls, are no longer thought of, and the time is passed in trifling, in laughter, in impertinent discourses. Dish succeeds dish, and to compensate for the absence of meat, the tables are covered with monstrous fishes in double rows, and when you have satisfied yourself with the first, the second is presented unto you, and you no longer remember you have partaken of the former, for it is the art of the cook to season them in such a manner, by diversity of sauces adapted to the different kinds of fish, that after having devoured five or six platefuls, satiety still leaves appetite undiminished. . . . To speak only of eggs, who can enumerate the various modes of dressing them? . . . As to water beverage, what can I say about it, when the common beverage is wine not even diluted with water. . . . On festival days we are not content to take ordinary wine, we must have foreign wine mixed up with other liquors. . . . Our markets scarcely afford stuffs rich enough for our taste."*

This luxury in the monasteries was often accompanied by very great immorality, and frequently the cloistered houses were more like

* St. Bernard's "Apology to Abbot William."

castles than monasteries, and resounded with the tramp of armed men, and with the instruments and voices of minstrels, buffoons, and women of light character. It is evident that a man full of holy purposes, as St. Bernard was, could not be tempted to enter places such as these. It was not to the rich and magnificent abbey, where the rule of St. Benedict was scarce thought of, that he and his little band of friends turned their eyes, but to a poor and struggling settlement which had lately sprung up as a protest against the prevailing luxury and corruption. This was the convent of Citeaux (or Cisteaux), situate in a barren wilderness in the diocese of Châlons-sur-Saône, and founded in the year 1098 by Robert, a nobleman of Champagne, in order to revive the primitive strictness of the Benedictine rule. To this monastery, then presided over by Stephen Harding, an Englishman, Bernard retired with more than thirty associates in the year 1113. The order which he joined became afterwards one of the most famous monastic orders, under the name of *Cistercians*, from the place where the first monastery was founded. It was distinguished from the older Benedictines by adopting a white dress instead of the black one which they wore, but it was still more distinguished by enforcing the rule that all monks should labour with their own hands in the fields, that they should live on the coarsest diet and the fewest possible meals, that their buildings, even their churches, should be most plain and homely, and most meanly furnished, and that all their life should be hard, painful, and ascetic. In fact, the whole of the Cistercian system was intended as a protest against and a reproof of the excessive luxury into which the Benedictines had fallen.

When Bernard with his thirty associates joined the first monastery of this new order, he at once brought to it an immense advance in power and influence. He, and many of his companions, were of noble birth, and extensively known, and it was thought to be a most edifying thing for this band of young noblemen to be seen engaged in hard toil in the fields, and in living such a mortified and self-denying life. Thus many votaries were soon brought to Citeaux, and the convent became quite unable to accommodate those who sought admission. The Abbot Stephen then determined to found a new house, in connection with Citeaux, and he selected a place called Clairvaux, which had been given to him for the purpose, and which was well suited for the sort of life which the monks desired. It was a wild and desolate spot in the bishopric of Langres, where strangers were not likely to penetrate, and where there was plenty of hard work to be had in tilling the unfruitful soil.

Of this new abbey, Bernard, though only in his twenty-sixth year, was chosen abbot, and his name has made the Convent of Clairvaux illustrious through all ages. The young abbot was so emaciated in appearance, that he looked scarce a living man, though his eyes burnt with a fire which could not be quenched. His austerities had ruined his health, and were nearly putting an end to his usefulness; and it is only just to say, that Bernard in after life lamented and condemned this excess of youthful zeal, which might have prematurely cut short his great career.

The fame of Bernard was now everywhere spread abroad, and many persons of all ranks came to him for counsel and instruction. Even by those in the highest positions, the opinion and judgment of a man who was thought to hold special converse with the unseen world were eagerly sought, and almost from his taking possession of his Abbey of Clairvaux, Bernard's time was, throughout his life, constantly occupied in the management and direction of important affairs in Church and State. A man of his purity, holiness, and force of character was urgently needed as a reformer; such manifold abuses then prevailed everywhere, and especially among the higher ecclesiastics. It was in order to amend these abuses, that Bernard composed his book "On the Conduct and Calling of Bishops." In this he first draws the character of a true priest, who by a genuine spiritual life becomes an example to his flock. Then he goes on to rebuke the opposite errors and abuses: the pomp of the clergy, especially in their dress; the costly foreign furs worn by them, their horse furniture decorated with the richest ornaments, and glittering with gold. Schoolboys and beardless youths, he said, were promoted to the episcopal office, and all seemed to be bent only on obtaining advance of dignities. Abbots were eager to purchase privileges and exemptions from the Pope, and the great object and origin of the pastoral office seemed to be lost sight of.

While he thus severely rebuked his own order,

Bernard also did not spare the great ones in the State. The King of France had acted unjustly towards some of his bishops, in laying hands on the property of their sees; Bernard severely denounced and threatened him. King Louis, however, would not yield, but continued his oppressions. The bishops then took a strange way of revenging themselves. They joined together to lay the kingdom under an interdict; that is to say, because the King was unjust, therefore all the private Christians of the land were to be refused the offices of religion, the churches were to be shut up, and the dead remain without Christian burial. That Christian pastors should act thus unchristianly, rather than submit to the spoiling of their goods, is indeed sad; but it is sadder still to find one so good and great as Bernard supporting them in this proceeding, by all the interest which he had with the Pope; and this is one of those instances in which it seems that provided he held the end to be good, Bernard was not sufficiently careful about the means employed. On this occasion the Pope had first espoused the cause of the King of France, and Bernard, indignant at this, had used some very plain language to the Court of Rome. "The Court of Rome," he exclaimed, "ever gives judgment according to the wishes of those who are present, rather than the rights of those who are absent."

That zeal which led men to devote their arms and their lives to the attempt to drive the infidel from the Holy Land, had a constant and ardent supporter in Bernard. About this time (1118), nine men of illustrious descent united for the purpose of keeping the way to the Holy Sepulchre open to pilgrims, and consecrating their lives for this purpose, took the vows of chastity, poverty, and obedience, before the Patriarch of Jerusalem. They established themselves near the site of the ancient Temple of Solomon, and hence were called Knights of the Temple, or Templars. The order rapidly increased, and Bernard, being appealed to by the chief, wrote a book to encourage and stimulate its spirit, called the "Commendation of the New Order of Knighthood." In this book occurs the strange sentiment, that unbelievers may be put to death, when there is no other means of restraining them from grievously disturbing the Christians. He lauds greatly the object which the Templars had in view, praises the poverty and simplicity which the order at first affected, and speaks of the vast multitude of criminals, profane, sacrilegious and abandoned persons who were flocking to join them, and on whose lives this new influence produced the best effects.

The most distinguished abbot of the Benedictines then living in France was Peter, called the Venerable, Abbot of Clugni. This abbey was very rich and magnificently appointed, but there had been some attempts made at reform here also, and sufficient variation from the ordinary usages of the Black Monks, to make Clugni and its dependent houses be regarded as an order by themselves, which was called the Clugniac order. But there was a wide difference between the reform that was attempted by the Cistercians and that of the Clugniacs. The latter allowed great ease and comfort to the monks, while it insisted on much attention being given to sacred study, and to grand religious services. The Cistercian required the monks, instead of studying, to be working hard in the fields, and would not allow any pomp in the services, nor any ornaments in the churches. The two great leaders of these competing systems consequently soon came into collision, and a sharp controversy was carried on between Peter and Bernard. Both were good men, and they mutually respected one another, but they nevertheless wrote very sharply.

Bernard admits and censures the pride and exaltation produced by asceticism in the Cistercians. "Is not humility in sables," he says, "better than arrogance in a monk's habit? The outward practices enjoined by the rule are not indeed to be neglected, but the hidden man of the soul—piety—these are the essentials without which all the rest profiteth nothing." But while he writes thus, he also denounces with extreme bitterness the pomp and luxury of the Clugniacs. He declares that he himself had seen an abbot with a train of sixty horses, "so that the spectators must have taken him for a sovereign prince rather than a pastor." He testifies against the decorations and works of art which were to be found in the churches of the Clugniacs. Their oratories covered with ornament and curious paintings, and all their ritual pomp recalled, he said, the ceremonial worship of the Jews.

Peter defends the changes that had been made in the original simplicity of the rule by the permission of authorities, and he declares that these outward things are not of so much importance as the inward rule, which is love. He says to Bernard: "Thou keepest the hard commands of Christ in fasting, watching, weariness and labour, and yet thou disregardest that easy one of love." He complains that the Cistercian monks will not receive the Clugniacs in their convents, and that they show their contempt of them in an unchristian and pharisaical manner.

There can be no doubt that though Peter may have displayed more of common sense and charity in this controversy, yet Bernard's views were much more in accordance with the original notion of what a monk ought to be. Strange that within a short period the monasteries of the order which professed such strictness should have become the most luxurious of any.

We now come to an important period in Bernard's life, when he was brought into close connection with the Pope, and by this means with all the sovereigns of Europe. There are numerous instances in the history of the Roman bishops of double elections to the occupancy of the chair of St. Peter, and of long-continued and unhappy schisms caused by this, some kings and bishops supporting one claimant, and others his rival. Such a division took place in the time of St. Bernard. On the death of Honorius some of the cardinals met secretly, and elected the Pope, who took the name of Innocent II., while others, declaring the election unlawful, elected Anacletus. Innocent appealed to the King of France to establish his claim, and the King ordered a meeting of the French bishops, to enquire into the matter. At this meeting Bernard was invited to attend, and as he believed that Innocent was the better man of the two, and more likely to be useful to the Church, he vigorously supported him. The French bishops were all convinced by his eloquence, and the King of France went to meet Innocent, who had come into his territories, and treated him with the greatest honour. Innocent then went into Germany, accompanied by Bernard, who had proved so useful a champion to his cause. At Luttich they met the German Emperor, and he being influenced in like manner, descended from his horse and conducted the Pope on foot into the cathedral, holding before him the staff of command. The same success attended Bernard's efforts in Italy, and mainly by the mighty influence which he had obtained Innocent was able to secure himself on his throne.

Such useful services as these naturally entitled Bernard to great power at the Court of Rome, which at this time was the tribunal which settled, or affected to settle, all disputes, both in the Church and State. Accordingly we find Bernard appealed to from all quarters, and able at his will to effect the greatest things. He could not indeed change the evil passions of men's hearts. He could not prevent King Louis from committing gross injustice and acts of cruelty, neither could he prevent his friend the Pope from resorting to the wicked and unchristian measure of laying France under an interdict; but he boldly protested against these and similar iniquitous proceedings. He told the King that he had been prompted by the devil to the deeds of blood and fire of which he had been guilty towards his people, and he plainly declared to the Pope that the Court of Rome, over which he ruled, was the chief source of injustice and confusion. "You receive," he says, "with open arms, the disorderly and litigious of all congregations, even the unruly and expelled members of the monastic establishments, who, in their return from your court, publicly boast of having found protection where they should rather have found punishment."

These protests and remonstrances have been put forth by good men in every age of the Church against the corruptions and abuses which have ever been dominant at Rome. But while Bernard denounced, as our own Bishop Grosseteste did, the injustice of the Roman Court, he also, like Grosseteste, helped to uphold the system, by attributing to one particular bishop an absolute authority over all the Church. This usurped power was certain to lead to the gross abuses of which these good men complained.

The Pope who succeeded Innocent was a man of peace, but then there came one who sought to establish his authority by arms, and while besieging the capitol in person, received a wound, of which he died—truly an incongruous end for a Christian bishop, and one who called himself the vicar of Christ.

The next Pope that was chosen was still more closely connected with Bernard than Innocent had been, and his influence at Rome now rose to the highest pitch. The choice of the cardinals fell upon one who was the abbot of a Roman convent, but who had been a monk in Bernard's own monastery of Clairvaux. He was elected pope under the name of Eugenius.

Bernard's first thought was that Eugenius was altogether unfit for the arduous post, which indeed required more than human strength to administer it aright. The Roman citizens were in rebellion against their ecclesiastical governor, as they very frequently were, and difficulties were on every side. Bernard, however, determined to lend his best aid to the new Pope to help him to perform his office. He addressed to him a letter full of noble sentiments, exhorting him to holiness of life and the practice of disinterested justice, that in which the Popes had usually fallen so terribly short.

When Eugenius was shortly afterwards driven from his capital city, Bernard addressed a sharp expostulation to the citizens of Rome, and as they paid no regard to his words, he called upon the German Emperor to invade Italy, in order to establish the Pope at Rome. It is very curious to observe here how completely Bernard was possessed with the idea that he had a mission to direct all the chief affairs of Church and State, and the deep obligation under which the Pope was placed to him, and the great reputation which he possessed for sanctity, seemed to lead every one to admit the claims which he made. His vast influence was now to be shown in a more signal and remarkable manner than it had yet been, and kings and emperors were to be exhibited as obedient servants at his command. The first great expedition made by Christian Europe to recover the Holy Land out of the hand of the infidel had been successful, and a Christian kingdom had been established at Jerusalem. Besides the sacred city, Edessa and Antioch in Syria, places of great importance for the support of the Christian power in the East, had also been captured by the crusaders, and held by them now for upwards of forty years. But in the year 1144 Europe received the terrible news that Edessa had been taken by the Sultan of Bagdad, after a great slaughter of the Christians, and that Antioch and Jerusalem itself were in danger of capture. An intense excitement was created by this intelligence. Men, remembering the triumphs of the first crusade, and looking upon the Holy Land as now won for Christianity, could not bear the notion of again losing it, and of the hated Crescent again triumphing over the Cross.

None was more deeply moved by the danger than Bernard, and he at once prepared to procure succour for the endangered Christians of the East. King Louis of France was naturally the first to whom he hurried, and it happened that at that time he was in a frame of mind most suitable for being influenced in the way which Bernard desired. He was preyed upon by bitter remorse for a great act of cruelty he had committed at Vitry, in burning 1,300 helpless persons in a church, and according to the custom of those days, he was anxious to do some meritorious act by way of expiation of his guilt. Bernard told him that no act could be so meritorious as making war upon the infidel, and King Louis at once agreed to undertake the expedition.

At Easter 1146 a vast assembly of the nobles of France was held at Vezelai. The King mounted a high platform, wearing the cross and having by his side the Abbot Bernard. The great orator was called upon to address the assembly, and with words of burning power he pressed upon them the holy duty of making war upon the enemies of the Cross. Christ, he declared, had suffered a second time at the hands of the infidel, and all who loved Him would buckle on the sword and go to the rescue. The words of Bernard produced an intense effect. The assembled multitude rent the air with shouts of " The cross ! The cross ! " and thronged around the scaffold to receive the sacred emblem from his hands, which, in the words of an eye-witness, he might rather be said to scatter than to distribute to them. The whole supply of crosses prepared for the occasion being exhausted, Bernard was obliged to tear up his own garments to supply the deficiency. The enthusiasm went on spreading, and the whole of France was possessed by it. From France it spread to the neighbourhood of the Rhine, and here the excitement of the people led them to break out into dreadful cruelties against the Jews. This wickedness Bernard severely rebuked, and by his great influence was enabled to check it. He next proceeded to try his power of persuasion upon the Emperor of Germany. He was admitted to preach before Conrad, and he drew a vivid picture of the Day of Judgment, and of the fate of those who should have refused to minister to Christ after all that they had received from Him. The Emperor was moved to tears, and exclaiming that he acknowledged the mercies of God, and desired to show himself worthy of them, declared that he accepted the crusade. A universal shout of joy arose, and Emperor and nobles received the Cross.

The efforts of Bernard were all approved of and supported by his friend Pope Eugenius; and he did not relax in his zeal and earnestness until he had seen two vast armies, one under the Emperor of Germany and the other under the King of France, set forth triumphantly towards the Holy Land. The miserable fate which overtook these great armies, the sacrifice of so many brave men and of such a vast amount of treasure, their utter failure in doing anything to help the Christian cause in the East, and the entire falsification of all Bernard's prophecies, would have overwhelmed any other man but him in disgrace and ruin. But the consideration which he enjoyed was enough to support even this. The failure of the crusade which he originated was attributed by him to the vices of those who were engaged in it, and by this easy method he saved his credit and still continued to be the oracle of Christendom. And this he continued to be throughout his career, to an extent never before attained by any man in a private station. He not only directed popes, kings, and emperors in their actions, he also directed men's opinions, condemned whom he pleased as heretics, and fashioned the religious thought of his day.

The time in which Bernard lived was one of much speculation on religious matters. The centuries before had been darker and more ignorant, but in the twelfth century men began to think and write more freely. The most remarkable of the free enquirers and bold questioners of the received opinions in religion were a scholar named Abélard, and a follower of his called Arnold of Brescia. Abélard was a man of great powers as a disputant, and when Bernard declared against his opinions, he was eager to dispute the points controverted between them Bernard met him at a Council held at Sens, not so much to dispute as to order the condemnation of his writings, all the bishops there assembled being humble servants at his direction. Abélard then appealed to the Pope, but this was like appealing from Bernard to Bernard,* as the Pope was completely under Bernard's influence. Bernard at once writes to him to direct that he

* Milman, "Lat. Christianity," iii. 374.

shall condemn these new opinions. The style in which he addresses one who was considered the head of Christendom is remarkable:—"For what has God raised thee up, lowly as thou wert in thine own eyes, and placed thee above kings and nations? Not that thou shouldst destroy, but that thou shouldst build up the faith. God has stirred up the fury of the schismatics, that thou mightest have the glory of crushing it." Accordingly Abélard and Arnold were condemned at once by the Pope.

It is especially for the stand which he took against the opinions of Abélard and his followers that Bernard is usually known by the name of the Last of the Fathers. The great writers after his time are generally called " the Schoolmen." They looked at religious truths in a way altogether different from that in which the earlier Christian Fathers and St. Bernard viewed them. These latter regard religious truths in a devotional way; they do not trouble themselves in trying to explain and prove them. They are not offended by difficulties and improbabilities; they teach that faith should be unquestioning, deep, and, as it were, blind. But writers like Abélard and the Schoolmen scan, question, and examine everything. Even the most difficult and mysterious doctrines are thought capable of explanation and proof. The one class of writers are for implicit faith, the other for pure reason. The truth, as usual, lies between the two. It was no doubt safer for persons of uninstructed and ordinary minds to be followers of Bernard than of Abélard; to receive all that the Church taught, however unreasonable some of it might be, rather than by raising questions about everything, to run the danger of causing shipwreck to their faith altogether.

The authority of Bernard availed to stop for a time the rationalistic movement; it was now to be tried against a movement of another sort. In the twelfth century there was a very general feeling throughout Europe against the luxury and careless lives of the clergy, which was often accompanied by ignorance and tyranny. We have seen that Bernard himself spoke most strongly on this point, but Bernard never thought of leading the people to rebel against the clergy; his words were addressed to the clergy themselves, not to their flocks. There were others, however, who thought it their duty to preach open war against the whole Church system, on the ground

Y

of the corruption of the clergy, and among these the most remarkable was Henry the Deacon. This man, who was gifted with great eloquence, preached throughout France, denouncing the clergy and many of the doctrines which they had added to the Scriptures. In the south, about Toulouse, his influence was astonishing. Bernard describes the state of things:—"The churches are without congregations, the congregations without a priest; the priests are no longer treated with the reverence due to them; the sanctuary of the Lord is no longer held sacred; the sacraments are no longer reverenced, the festivals no longer observed. Men die in their sins, and souls are hurried before the awful judgment-seat of God without having been reconciled to Him by penance or strengthened by the Supper of the Lord. The way to Christ is closed against the children of Christians, the grace of baptism is denied, and those whom the Saviour called to Him with fatherly love, 'Suffer the little children to come unto Me,' are no longer permitted to draw nigh Heaven."

The influence of Henry the Deacon was so great that the Pope, terrified by its effects, despatched a bishop with a special commission to oppose it. The Pope's legate was received by the people in the south of France with contempt and derision, and none seemed inclined to desert their new teacher at his instance. Then the legate bethought of sending for the great preacher of the day, the man who by his force of character was able to overcome all obstacles. In two days' time Bernard made his appearance at Toulouse, in mean apparel, with haggard countenance, so that none could accuse him of luxury and soft living. The people, knowing well his great reputation for holiness, received him with respect. Bernard mounted the pulpit and delivered a thrilling and heart-searching discourse. As he saw the people melted to tears by his words, he invited them to return to the unity of the Church, and desired that those who had received the word of salvation should hold up their right hands in token of their submission to the Catholic Church. At once the whole congregation raised their right hands.

Bernard thus for the present triumphed, but the effect produced by the teaching of Henry the Deacon did not altogether pass away. Fifty years after this the country in which Bernard had preached was swarming with sectaries professing very extravagant and dangerous doctrines, and called from Albi, one of their chief places of influence, Albigeois or Albigenses. Against these one of the most wicked and cruel wars recorded in history was waged at the instigation of the Pope of that day.

The glory and reputation which Bernard now enjoyed in the Church were brought to a climax when the Pope Eugenius, who, as has been said, was once a monk of Clairvaux under him, came to pay a visit to his former master at his old monastery and appeared again as a monk among the monks. What could have been more gratifying to Bernard and more calculated to raise him in the eyes of his contemporaries than such a tribute of respect from one who occupied so great a place.

The infirmities of age and the weakness of body which had all his days pursued him, were now making the termination of this great life to approach. Bernard sighed to be released, but while he was in the flesh he would be still occupied with useful labours. Accordingly he devoted the latter part of his life to the composition of a work intended to guide and direct his dear friend, Pope Eugenius. This book is called a

"Treatise on Consideration," and shows in a striking manner the ardent devotion which possessed Bernard's soul, and his high and exalted notion of the pastoral office, and how different it was from the way of life which was ordinary to the Popes. "You are surrounded," he writes to the Pope, "on all sides by noise and clamour, weighed down at all times with the yoke of your slavery. Did Paul make himself the servant of men for the purpose of ministering to their covetousness? Did the ambitious, the covetous, the sacrilegious, the unclean, and such like monsters of men, come flocking to Paul from the ends of the earth, to solicit or to retain ecclesiastical preferments through his Apostolical authority? What can be at once more slavish and more unbecoming a Pope than to be employed, not only every day, but every hour of the day, in such matters and for such men? Which power and authority seems to you the greater, that of forgiving sins or that of dividing goods?"

Not that Bernard went so far as to advise the Pope to hear no appeals and to judge no causes. The custom of the times in a measure forced this upon the Bishop of Rome. But he would have him think the spiritual part of his office of the chief importance. " Gold, silver, and dominions," he writes, " may be obtained by other means, but not by virtue of any Apostolical right; for the Apostle could not bequeath what he did not possess; he transmitted to you what he himself had—the care of the Church."

Certainly the venal character of the Court of Rome, the state and pomp which it was the custom for the Pope to affect, and all the abuses of the system, could not have been more strongly denounced by one who was a bitter foe to the papacy than they were by Bernard, who was its fast and true friend. " Show me, if you can," he says, " one man in your great and vast city who recognises your authority without being prompted by gain, or by the hope of gain. You who are appointed to be a shepherd of souls go about among them decked with gold, and with a variety of pompous apparel, and what do your flock receive? Such conduct, I would say if I dared, is more befitting a shepherd of devils than of sheep."

Having thus condemned the pomp and worldliness which were prevalent at Rome, Bernard then enlarges upon heavenly contemplation and all the beauties and glories of true religion. His words breathe the true Divine spirit, and it was not unfitly said by one who was far from sympathising with Bernard's doctrine, that " in his book on ' Consideration,' Bernard speaks in such a strain that you might think Truth herself to be speaking " (Calvin).

In his last illness the words of Scripture were ever in his mouth. His whole demeanour was that of a man who had already begun to taste the glory that shall be revealed. His humility was great and unfeigned, his faith firm and bright. A short time before his death, when his sufferings had ceased to be lightened by sleep, he dictated these words to a friend :—" Pray to the Saviour, who willeth not the death of a sinner, that He delay not my departure, and yet that He will be pleased to guard it : support him that hath no merits of his own by your prayers, that the adversary of our salvation may not find any place open to his attacks."

We conclude this sketch by Luther's estimate of St. Bernard. " This," he writes, " did Bernard, a man so godly, so holy, so chaste that he is to be commended and preferred before all the Fathers. He, being grievously sick, and having no hope of life, put not his trust in his single life, wherein he had yet lived most chastely ; not in his good works and deeds of charity, whereof he had done many; but removing them far out of his sight, and receiving the benefit of Christ by faith, he said:—' I have lived wickedly, but thou, Lord Jesus, dost possess the kingdom of Heaven by double right; first, because Thou art the Son of God; secondly, because Thou hast purchased it by Thy death and passion. The first Thou keepest for Thyself as Thy birthright; the second Thou givest to me, not by the right of my works, but by the right of grace.' He set not against the wrath of God his own monkery nor his angelical life; but he took of that one thing which was necessary, and so was saved."*

* Luther on Galatians.

Society for Promoting Christian Knowledge.

PUBLICATIONS
ON THE CHRISTIAN EVIDENCES.

BOOKS

	Price.
	s. d.
MORAL DIFFICULTIES CONNECTED WITH THE BIBLE. Being the Boyle Lectures for 1871, preached in Her Majesty's Chapel at Whitehall. By the Rev. J. A. Hessey, D.C.L., preacher to the Hon. Society of Gray's Inn, &c. FIRST SERIES. Post 8vo............Cloth boards	1 6
MORAL DIFFICULTIES CONNECTED WITH THE BIBLE. Being the Boyle Lectures for 1872, preached in Her Majesty's Chapel at Whitehall. By the Rev. J. A. Hessey, D.C.L., Preacher to the Hon. Society of Gray's Inn, &c. SECOND SERIES. Post 8vo............Cloth boards	2 6
PRAYER AND RECENT DIFFICULTIES ABOUT IT. The Boyle Lectures for 1873, being the THIRD SERIES of "Moral Difficulties connected with the Bible." Preached in Her Majesty's Chapel at Whitehall. By the Rev. J. A. Hessey, D.C.L., Preacher to the Hon. Society of Gray's Inn, &c. Post 8vo............Cloth boards	2 6
THE ANALOGY OF RELIGION. Dialogues founded upon Butler's "Analogy of Religion." By Rev. H. R. Huckin, M.A., St. John's College, Oxford, one of the Masters at Merchant Taylors' School. Post 8vo. Cloth boards	3 0
"MIRACLES." By the Rev. E. A. Litton, M.A., Examining Chaplain of the Bishop of Durham. Crown 8vo................	1 6
HISTORICAL ILLUSTRATIONS OF THE OLD TESTAMENT. By the Rev. G. Rawlinson, M.A., Camden Professor of Ancient History, Oxford. Post 8vo. (Third Edition) ....Cloth boards	1 6
CAN WE BELIEVE IN MIRACLES? By G. Warington, Esq., of Caius College, Cambridge. Post 8vo ....Cloth boards	1 6
THE MORAL TEACHING OF THE NEW TESTAMENT VIEWED AS EVIDENTIAL TO ITS HISTORICAL TRUTH. By the Rev. C. A. Row. Post 8vo............ Cloth boards	1 6
SCRIPTURE DOCTRINE OF CREATION. By the Rev. T. R. Birks. Post 8vo............ Cloth boards	1 6
THE NORWICH DISCOURSES. By the Bishop of Peterborough, the Dean of Norwich, and the Lord Bishop of Derry. Nos. 1 to 10 in a Volume. Cloth boards	1 6
THOUGHTS ON THE FIRST PRINCIPLES OF THE POSITIVE PHILOSOPHY CONSIDERED IN RELATION TO THE HUMAN MIND. By Benjamin Shaw, M.A., Barrister-at-Law. Post 8vo. ....Limp cloth	0 8

Post 8vo.] (18/11/74.)

THOUGHTS ON THE BIBLE.
  By the Rev. W. Gresley. Post 8vo............*Cloth boards* 1 6

THE REASONABLENESS OF PRAYER.
  By the Rev. P. Onslow. Post 8vo.................*Limp cloth* 0 3

LOCKE ON THE EXISTENCE OF GOD.
  Post 8vo. ....*Paper cover* 0 3

PALEY'S EVIDENCES OF CHRISTIANITY.
  A New Edition, with Notes, Appendix, and Preface. By
  the Rev. E. A. Litton. Post 8vo. 4 0

THE STORY OF CREATION, AS TOLD BY THEOLOGY
  AND SCIENCE. By the Rev. T. S. Ackland, Vicar of
  Balne, near Selby, Yorkshire. Post 8vo.........*Cloth boards* 1 6

MAN'S ACCOUNTABLENESS FOR HIS RELIGIOUS
  BELIEF. A Lecture delivered at the Hall of Science, on
  Tuesday, April 2nd, 1872. By the Rev. Daniel Moore,
  Incumbent of Holy Trinity, Paddington. Post 8vo.
                                                    Paper cover 0 3

THE THEORY OF PRAYER: WITH SPECIAL REFER-
  ENCE TO MODERN THOUGHT. By the Rev. W. H.
  Karslake, M.A., Assistant Preacher at Lincoln's-Inn,
  Vicar of Westcott, Dorking, late Fellow and Tutor at
  Merton College, Oxford. Post 8vo....................*Limp cloth* 1 0

WHEN WAS THE PENTATEUCH WRITTEN?
  By George Warington, B.A., author of "Can we Believe
  in Miracles?" &c. Post 8vo...... .... *Cloth boards* 1 6

THE CREDIBILITY OF MYSTERIES.
  A Lecture delivered at St. George's Hall, Langham Place.
  By the Rev. Daniel Moore, M.A. Post 8vo. *Paper cover* 0 3

ANALOGY OF RELIGION, NATURAL AND REVEALED
  TO THE CONSTITUTION AND COURSE OF NATURE: to which
  are added, Two Brief Dissertations. By Bishop Butler,
                                                    Cloth boards 2 6

SHORT AND EASY METHOD WITH THE DEISTS;
  wherein the certainty of the Christian Religion is demonstrated by infallible proof: in a letter to a friend. To
  which are added, a Letter from the Author to a Deist, upon
  his conversion by reading his book: and the Truth Of
  Christianity demonstrated, in a Dialogue betwixt a Christian and a Deist; by the Rev. Charles Leslie. *Cloth boards* 1 0

WHY DO YOU BELIEVE THE BIBLE TO BE THE
  WORD OF GOD. An argument to prove the Divine Au-
  thority and Inspiration of Holy Scripture, by Josiah
  Bateman, M.A., &c. 12mo. .... *Cloth boards* 1 0

CHRISTIAN EVIDENCES:
  intended chiefly for the young, by the **Most Reverend
  Richard Whately, D.D.**, Archbishop of Dublin. 18mo.
            Cloth boards 1s., or 12mo., *Paper cover* 0 4

A MORAL DEMONSTRATION, showing that the
  Religion of Jesus Christ is from God. By Jeremy Taylor,
  D.D., Lord Bishop of Down and Connor. 32mo.
                                                    Limp cloth 0 3

PUBLICATIONS OF THE SOCIETY.

Price
s. d.

THE EFFICACY OF PRAYER.
By the Rev. W. H. Karslake, M.A., Assistant Morning Preacher at Lincoln's Inn, &c. &c. Post 8vo. *Limp cloth* 0 6

AN APOLOGY FOR THE BIBLE, in a Series of
Letters addressed to THOMAS PAINE. By the Right Rev. Richard Watson, D.D., late Lord Bishop of Llandaff 18mo. ....*Paper cover* 0 6

SCIENCE AND THE BIBLE: a Lecture by the Right
Rev. Chas. Perry, D.D., Lord Bishop of Melbourne. 18mo. *Paper cover* 4d., or *Limp cloth* 0 6

THE BIBLE: Its Evidences, Characteristics,
and Effects. A Lecture by the Right Rev. Charles Perry, D.D., Lord Bishop of Melbourne. 18mo. ...... *Paper cover* 0 4

INFIDELITY, in its Perilous Bearing on the
Present and the future State of Man. By the Rev. Hugh Stowell, M.A., of Manchester. 18mo. ....*Paper cover* 0 4

A SERMON ON THE EFFICACY OF PRAYER.
By the Right Reverend Harvey Goodwin, D.D., Bishop of Carlisle. 16mo..*Paper cover*, 0 2

THE TESTIMONY OF THE PRIMITIVE FATHERS
to the Truth of the Gospel History. By T. G. Bonney, B.D. Fellow of St. John's College, Cambridge, 18mo.
Paper cover 0 2

THE TRUTH OF THE GOSPEL HISTORY confirmed
by the Earliest Witnesses after Apostolic Times. A Lecture delivered at Potsdam, by the late Dr. F. W. Krummacher. Translated from the German. 18mo.
Paper cover 0 2

A LECTURE ON THE BIBLE, by the Very Rev.
E. M. Goulbourn, Dean of Norwich. 18mo. *Paper cover* 0 2

CHRISTIAN EVIDENCE IN A VERY SMALL COMPASS.
By Josiah W. Smith, B.C.L., Q.C. 32mo. ......*Paper cover* 0 1

TRACTS.

DIFFICULTIES OF OLD TESTAMENT CHARACTERS.

No. 7.—CAIN AND HIS TIMES. 12mo. ....per 100   2 0
No. 4.—THE FALL OF DAVID........................ per 100   2 0
No. 9.—ABRAHAM'S SACRIFICE .... „   2 0
No. 10.—DECEIT OF JACOB............................... „   2 0
No. 11.—CRUELTY OF JOSHUA . ... „   2 0
No. 12.—JEPHTHAH'S VOW. .... „   2 0

SCRIPTURE DIFFICULTIES.

No. 1.—THE CHARACTER OF NOAH. 12mo. per 100   1 0
No. 2.—JESUS CHRIST CAME TO SEND A SWORD
ON EARTH. By Ditto. 12mo............................per 100   3 0
No. 3.—COMMERCIAL SHARPNESS EXEMPLIFIED
and Exposed in the Parable of the Unjust Steward. By the Rev. F. Morse. 12mo. .... per 100   3 0

PUBLICATIONS OF THE SOCIETY.

	Price
	s. d.

No. 8.—Order, Adaptation, Design.
By the Rev. C. A. Row .... „ 2 0

No. 5.—Is There a God? Adapted from N.
Roussel, &c. 12mo. .... per 100 4 0

No. 6.—Norwich Cathedral Argumentative
Discourses in Defence of the Faith.

By the Lord Bishop of Peterborough.

Discourse 1. Christianity and Free Thought. 12mo. each	0	1
Discourse 2. Christianity and Scepticism. 12mo...... „	0	1
Discourse 3. Christianity and Faith. 12mo. .... „	0	1
Discourse 4. The Demonstration of the Spirit. 12mo. „	0	1

By the Dean of Norwich.

Discourse 5. Above Reason, not contrary to it. 12mo. „	0	1
Discourse 6. The Cumulative Argument in favour of Christianity. 12mo. .... „	0	1
Nos. 1 to 6 in a Volume........................Limp cloth	0	10

By the Lord Bishop of Derry.

Discourse 7. Man's Natural Life. 12mo................. „	0	1
Discourse 8. Man's Moral Life. 12mo. .... „	0	1
Discourse 9. Man's Wedded Life. 12mo.............. „	0	1
Discourse 10. Man's Fallen and Redeemed Life. 12mo. „	0	1

	Price per 100.
No.	s. d.

1581. Deserted House (The).
Some thoughts for thinkers 5 0

1703. General Credibility of Gospel History
(The) and Authenticity of the Gospels. An Instruction Tract. By the Rev. Mervyn Archdall. 12mo......... 0 4

1579. John Aked of Barnsley.
The Story of an Unbeliever 5 0

158. Letter to Adam Smith, LL.D., on the
life, death, and philosophy of his friend David Hume, Esq., by **Bishop Horne** 5 0

1523. Materialist Convicted (A). 4 0

1306. Miracles: a Conversation. 6 0

1547. Miracles, an Old Man's Thoughts
about. By the Rev. A. T. Craig, M.A. 2 0

940. Reasons for retaining Christianity.
Extracted from Bishop Watson's Letters to Gibbon 6 0

1365. Why does not God make me believe?
A Workshop Conversation 2 0

LONDON:
77, Great Queen Street, Lincoln's Inn Fields, W.C.;
4, Royal Exchange, E.C.; 48, Piccadilly, W.

www.ingramcontent.com/pod-product-compliance
Lightning Source LLC
Chambersburg PA
CBHW031426230426
43668CB00007B/450